ECONOMICS 101

ECONOMICS 101

AN ESSENTIAL GUIDE TO HOW THE ECONOMY WORKS

101

ELAINE SCHWARTZ

SIRIUS

ELAINE SCHWARTZ has spent her career sharing the interesting side of economics. At the Kent Place School in Summit, New Jersey, she has been honored through an Endowed Chair in Capitalism and the History Department chairmanship. At the same time, she has written several books including *Understanding Our Economy* (originally published by Addison Wesley as *Economics: Our American Economy*) and *Econ 101 ½* (Avon Books/Harper Perennial). Elaine has also written for the *Encyclopedia of New Jersey* (Rutgers University Press) and was a featured teacher in the Annenberg/CPB video project "The Economics Classroom." Beyond the classroom, she has also presented Econ 101 ½ talks, and developed economics curricula and led workshops for the Foundation for Teaching Economics, the Council on Economic Education, and the Concord Coalition. You can find more of her writing at https://econlife.com where she combines economics, current events, and history in a daily blog.

SIRIUS

This edition published in 2024 by Sirius Publishing, a division of
Arcturus Publishing Limited,
26/27 Bickels Yard, 151–153 Bermondsey Street,
London SE1 3HA

ISBN: 978-1-3988-3651-8
AD011709US

Printed in Malaysia

CONTENTS

INTRODUCTION

How you see the world depends on the lens you wear. If you wanted to focus on the past, your lens would see history; with human behavior, it could be psychology; for money, you might expect to see economics.

Yes? Not entirely.

More than money, economics is about cost. If you are watching Hulu, the "cost" could be Netflix or Disney+. If you grow wheat, the "cost" might have been a barley field. Because economists define cost as the sacrificed alternative, all decisions have a cost. They always require a trade-off.

So, when we ask what we mean by economics, we know we mean cost. But the cost of what? Economics is all about the cost of producing and distributing our goods and services. If a government builds roads, it has less for education. Similarly, spending eight hours in the office has the cost of more leisure time at home. Indeed, whether you are looking at the big picture through macroeconomics, or at smaller units with microeconomics, we see everywhere that decisions require trade-offs that have a cost.

With cost as our foundation, we will explore economics.

From there, we will see how different economic systems manage production and distribution. We will see how millions of consumers in a market are nudged by an invisible hand that encourages them to spend less when prices are high and more when they are low. As for government, we will see monetary policy and the spending, taxes, and borrowing that comprise fiscal policy.

And yet, what we see still will not be complete until we focus on the market's challenges. Ranging from sustainability to inequality, the issues that let us look backward at what we have created will let us look ahead to what we want.

Like a jigsaw puzzle composed of many stories and ideas, a picture of economics will gradually emerge. It will be an image that demonstrates how economics touches us at home, at work, and through government. Wearing our economic lenses, we will see that we are really just looking at our everyday lives.

So, let's begin…

Chapter One
TRADE-OFFS AND MARGINS

*A Model of the Economy—
Scarcity—Land, Labor, and Capital—
Trade-offs—Margins*

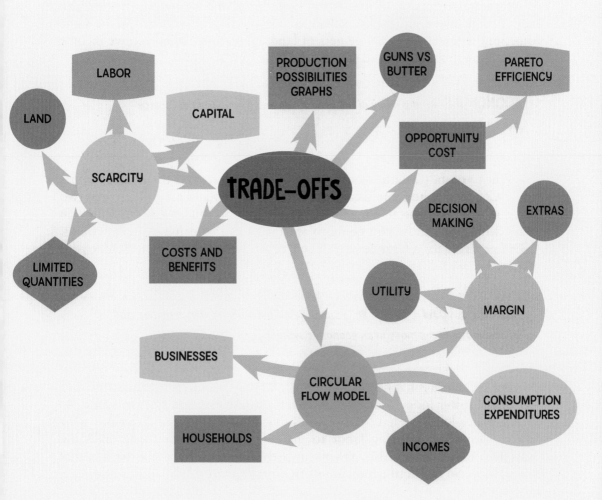

Our first look at economics will take us to a model of our economy and the trade-offs that every decision requires. We will see that we are frequently making trade-offs at a margin where we do a little more or a little less.

A MODEL OF THE ECONOMY

Our story starts with a latte.

Imagine for a moment that you make a morning stop at a Starbucks. An economist would say that you have entered a model of a market economy.

Representing a minimal role for government, the model (see next page) displays the interaction of millions of households and businesses. It shows an upper loop, where money is exchanged for goods and services. At the same time, in the lower loop, the owners of land, labor, and capital receive income for creating those goods and services.

ECONOMICS ▶ *the study of the production and distribution of "scarce" land, labor, and capital.*

When you buy a latte, you've actually strolled around the model's upper loop. Connecting households and businesses, the model's arrows move in two directions. They illustrate the money you bring to Starbucks and the drink you leave with. They show you going to Starbucks and agreeing to pay, perhaps, $3.65 or £3.10 for a Grande latte. Then, reversing direction, they display your departure.

CIRCULAR FLOW MODEL ▶ *a simplified illustration of where money, and goods and services move in an economic system.*

But still more is happening.

In the lower loop, your barista leaves a household and goes to work. As in the upper loop, we have two arrows that flow in opposite directions. One arrow shows her bringing labor to the café while the other one takes her paycheck to her home. Also, as you can see, more than labor gets paid in that lower loop. So too do the individuals that provide their land and capital.

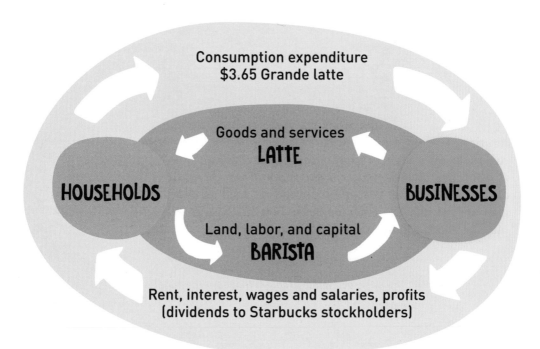

The Model

In addition to one household and a Starbucks, the circular flow model can represent all households and businesses. Defining a household as where people live alone, with family, or with unrelated individuals, in the US there are around 123 million households, 28 million for the UK, 197 million for the European Union (EU), and, in Japan, close to 53.3 million. Similarly, the Businesses sector is really close to 41 million business establishments in the US, 5.6 million in the UK, approximately 25.9 million in the EU, and 20.5 million in Japan. As a result, your upper loop stroll might not have taken you to Starbucks. Instead, with countless possibilities, you could have gone to another coffee shop or visited one online. Correspondingly, in the creation of your purchases the factors of production—the land, labor, and capital—were in the lower loop.

SCARCITY

Next, having moved through an upper loop of purchases and a lower loop with production, we can consider the problem that the circular flow solves. The problem is scarcity.

Defined as a limited quantity of goods and services, scarcity is not about shortages. It just means that when we push aside all of economics' complexities, we are looking at the decisions we make to produce and distribute a limited quantity of goods and services. Our community, our nation, and the world have to decide who gets what because everyone can't have everything.

There are countless alternative ways to decide who gets what because of scarcity. Some argue that merit should be used as allocation criteria. Others advocate an equal system solely based on citizenship. A third possible answer could be allocation decisions that support the least advantaged.

SCARCITY ▶ the basic economic problem that says the supply of all goods and services is limited.

AN ECONOMIC EXTRA
In 1982, Starbucks hired a Brooklyn-born thermos salesman as its new marketing chief. Destined to become an entrepreneurial legend, Howard Schultz's big moment came when he attended an international housewares show in Milan, Italy. He tried an espresso at one of Milan's 1,500 espresso bars, and then enjoyed his first latte in Verona. Convinced that Americans could be persuaded to love these "new" styles of coffee, he bought himself six Starbucks franchises and a coffee-roasting plant. The rest is coffee history.

Howard Schultz, the founder of Starbucks.

PARETO EFFICIENCY ▶ *when any further allocation of a commodity will make someone worse off if someone else becomes better off.*

Yet another alternative involves recognizing how making one group better can harm others. This is known as Pareto Efficiency, and we can use a shared eight-slice pizza as an example. However you divide it (4 and 4; 3 and 5; 7 and 1), when someone gives a slice to another individual, they are worse off because the other person got more. Considering Pareto Efficiency generally (and far beyond pizza), we can ponder how our scarcity decisions could exacerbate inequality.

All of these decisions return us to a second basic economic principle: that the lens through which we look at things can be either macroeconomic or microeconomic. Focusing on the big picture, macro includes policies that affect everyone's employment, the price level, and economic growth. Meanwhile, micro concentrates on you, me, our households, and our businesses.

MACROECONOMICS ▶ *the study of economics through big issues that include an entire nation's monetary (money supply and credit) and fiscal (spending, taxing, borrowing) policies.*

Whether looking down from the top at big groups, or up from the bottom at smaller entities, we see scarcity everywhere. On the national level, spending more on one program means we spend less on another one. Closer to home, supermarkets that contain more frozen foods could have less space for fresh produce. On the macro and micro levels, always making choices, we consistently accept sacrificed alternatives—a cost—because of scarcity. The market, on which we will concentrate, provides one of many possible solutions.

MICROECONOMICS ▶ *the study of economics from the bottom up that would include households, supply and demand, and how individual business firms behave.*

LAND, LABOR, AND CAPITAL

So, whether looking at a Starbucks, a supermarket, or any of our model's millions of businesses, we see a limited supply of the land, labor, and capital that we use to create all of our goods and services. Called the factors of production, land, labor, and capital populate the lower loop of our circular flow model.

THE FACTORS OF PRODUCTION

LAND

Land includes all natural resources. It could be a stream, a lake, or a river, a large tract of farmland or prime real estate. It also encompasses other natural resources, such as untouched trees, undiscovered oil and gas reserves, and gold.

LABOR

Labor is the effort that people devote to a task. Our supermarket shelves were filled by labor. Labor ran a mechanized dairy farm that created the milk in our latte and managed the Starbucks where we purchased it. In addition, entrepreneurs are a special kind of labor. As the innovators who create new kinds of businesses, in the circular flow, they are crucial for growth and development.

CAPITAL

Capital refers to the assets used to make us more productive. It can take many forms. Physical capital includes buildings, tools, equipment, and inventory. The coffee machines at Starbucks are physical capital as is a supermarket freezer and its self-checkout equipment. To this we can add the human capital that is made of the on-the-job training and education that similarly elevate our productivity. Just as we stock tools in a factory, knowledge accumulates in the people that work for a local Starbucks, our supermarkets, and all other businesses.

TRADE-OFFS

At this point, an economist would remind us that scarcity makes us decide what we do and do not want. And once we make a choice, that means we have sacrificed an alternative. More broccoli means less asparagus. Having pizza for lunch, you did not select a sandwich. If we rejected a market economy, then we needed another system. Each decision required a trade-off. Choosing was refusing.

Opportunity Cost

What you refuse is called the opportunity cost of the decision. We can use an opportunity cost table to make a decision. By naming the benefits taken and the benefits forgone by a decision, this table tells what we gain and what we lose. Every decision has an opportunity cost because for every decision there was a sacrificed alternative—what you did not do. By going to Starbucks, the opportunity cost was McDonald's—not McDonald's benefits.

Alternatives	Go to Starbucks	Go to McDonald's
Benefits	Enjoy latte	Enjoy Big Mac
Decision	Starbucks	
Opportunity cost		McDonald's
Benefits forgone	Enjoy Big Mac	

Production Possibilities Graphs

Production possibilities graphs are another way to see trade-offs. They show the most a country, a business, a person (or another entity) can produce, illustrating a menu of choices. When you use your land, labor, and capital for wheat, you have nothing left for barley. While more for wheat means less barley, you are still using the three resources that compose your factors of production. As you can see, our production possibilities are all about trade-offs.

Guns vs Butter

The classic production possibilities (PP) graph illustrates the choice between guns and butter. By guns, we really mean military goods and services, while butter is all of the things that consumers want and need. Because of "scarce" (limited) land, labor, and capital, more of one necessitates less of the other. It means that by adding 8 guns we lose 1 butter (from 15 to 14). Then, to move up to 14 guns, we sacrifice 2 butters (to 12). An economist would say that the cost of 8 guns is 1 butter. Similarly, 6 more guns will cost us 2 butters.

A menu of production possibilities shows the cost when we make more of one item. Moving from 0 to 8 guns will cost us 1 butter.

On a graph, we see a choice between the two commodities. Moving up the curve, you have more butter, while the opportunity cost (the sacrifice) is more guns. Traveling in the other direction, you sacrifice an increasing amount of butter.

Guns	Butter
0	15
8	14
14	12
18	9
20	5
21	0

OPPORTUNITY COST ▶ *the most desirable sacrificed alternative created by a decision.*

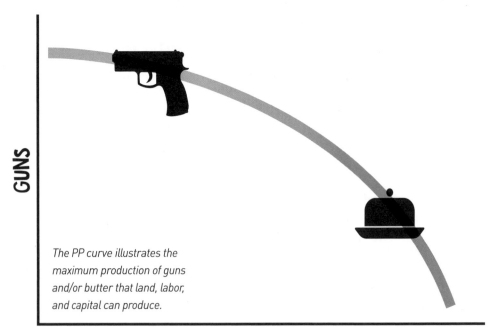

GUNS

The PP curve illustrates the maximum production of guns and/or butter that land, labor, and capital can produce.

BUTTER

Efficiency

In addition to a line, a production possibilities graph can have a dot that identifies the level of current production. Drawn on the line, the dot says that production is the most it could be. Moving inside the line, the dot's message is underutilization—a signal that we could make more.

The reasons for underutilization can range from weather to war to the economic system. They could include afternoon siestas and prejudicial behavior.

When we add a dot to a production possibilities graph, we see how the economy is performing at a moment in time. While dots on the curve show the most that can be produced, the dot on this graph displays underutilization.

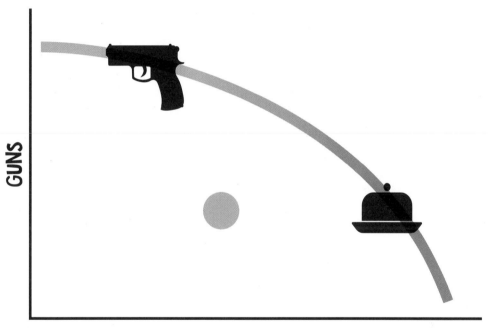

Showing underutilization, the dot could reflect the impact of unemployment or a natural disaster.

Growth

Let's assume that your country acquires land, or it welcomes new immigrants, or an entrepreneur invents a new technology. The result is new land, labor, or capital that creates growth. On a production possibilities graph, the line moves to the right. Meanwhile, a disaster that permanently diminishes the country's land, labor, or capital moves the line to the left.

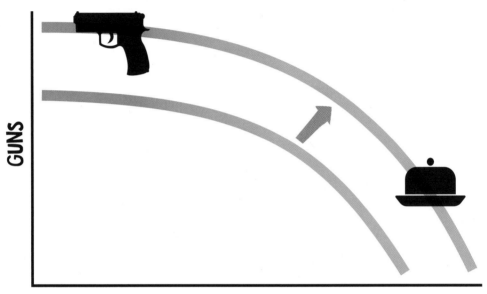

To show that an economy is capable of producing more than in
the past, we just need to shift the curve to the right.

Cost

There is a reason that most production possibilities curves bow outward. To see why, we just need to think about increasing cost and planting almonds or corn. Assume that growing one almond requires 1.1 gallons (5 liters) of water. If we want more almonds, at first we shift the best-irrigated land from corn production to almonds. But if we want even more, then it is increasingly difficult to find the additional water we need and create the capital that supplies it. Because we need more resources to get the same output, the cost (the sacrifice) in corn resources is greater. As a result, the curve bows outward.

It is also possible—though not likely—that the cost will be constant. With constant costs, the decrease of one item is always the same number. A third possibility that is even more unlikely (usually impossible) is zero cost. Then, the quantity of one commodity remains constant as the other increases.

MARGINS

Talking about increases and decreases takes us to the basic economic idea that says, at an imaginary margin, we usually do a little more or less. Picture for a moment a piece of paper with a margin. Telling us how much extra space we can access, the margin can move a little to the left or to the right. It is a dividing line between what we use and what is available to us.

An almond farm.

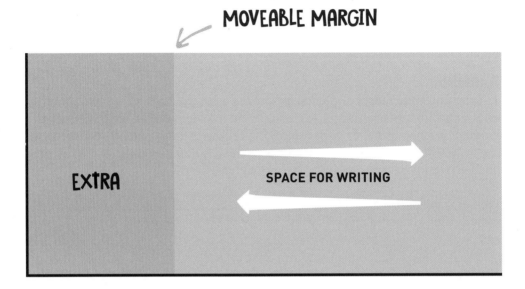

Similarly, when you hit the Snooze button on your alarm clock, you have made a decision at the margin for more sleep. Or, if you exceed the speed limit while driving, you have made a decision at the margin to go faster. When governments decide to distribute more vaccines during a pandemic, it is a decision that has been made at the margin.

Individual Decisions at the Margin

Because the position of a margin acts as an incentive, it can nudge us toward a certain decision about our extras. When you make an everyday parking decision, you are at the margin. It is possible that every time you drive to work, parking costs you $15. Instead, though, you might have purchased a monthly pass for $300. With the first alternative, during the month the daily margin is at $15. But with the monthly option, the daily margin is zero. At the beginning of another month, it will again be $300. But within the month, the extra parking does not cost anything extra.

You can see that your incentives at each margin are very different. If you pay $15 each time you park, you might decide to stay home and save the money. However, having paid $300 to park as many times as you want, your decision on whether to drive should not be affected (at least for this particular reason). You could even drive to lunch while at work.

Business Decisions at the Margin

In the lower loop of the circular flow, deciding how many people to hire, many might think of basing their decision on an average. Here again, we need to think at the margin.

> **MARGIN** ▶ *the imaginary divider that separates what you have from the extras you can add.*

In a hypothetical lemonade business (with oversimplified numbers), assume each worker costs an extra $20 an hour. If you earn a total of $190 from five workers, then each one averages $38—much more than the $20 marginal cost of the fifth worker. Should you conclude that the average tells you that you need your fifth worker?

NO.

Thinking at the margin takes us in a different direction. It tells us to compare the extra cost of each worker to the benefit they create. In the table overleaf, you can see that it makes no sense to hire worker #5, because their marginal cost is greater than the marginal revenue they generate. Paid $20, they create $15. As long as marginal revenue exceeds marginal cost, you keep hiring.

Businesses also think at the margin in the upper loop. Knowing that extras can become increasingly unattractive, Starbucks offers its Pumpkin Spice latte for a limited time during the fall. Similarly, we never know when a McDonald's McRib will appear and then be withdrawn. Both are removed from the menu because of reasons relating to their utility. With utility meaning usefulness or satisfaction, the marginal utility of subsequent lattes or McRibs decreases. Starbucks and McDonald's appear to know when they should take each item off the menu before diminishing marginal utility sets in—before the extras no longer taste as good as they did before.

> **UTILITY** ▶ *the usefulness or satisfaction obtained from a good or a service.*

# of workers	Total labor cost ($)	Extra labor cost ($) (marginal cost, MC)	Total revenue ($) (T)	Extra revenue ($) (marginal revenue, MR)	MR minus MC ($)
1	20	20	100		
2	40	20	130	30	10
3	60	20	155	25	5
4	80	20	175	20	0
5	100	20	190	15	-5

Government Decisions at the Margin

Finally, focusing our marginal lens on government, wherever we look we see something extra. Legislative debate always requires give and take. When proponents of a law want to cut costs, they know they can reduce the size of what they support, or erase entire programs and keep others. These are often motivated by political considerations, of course, but they involve cost sacrifices that are made at the margin, with choices about whether to have more or less extra, and making trade-offs.

Beginning with a circular flow visit to Starbucks and ending at the margin, we can see that economics is about much more than money. It takes us to the cost of what we do every day, to trade-offs, because there is never a free lunch; and to the margin, where we make our decisions.

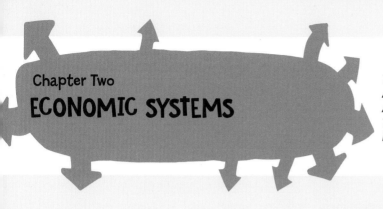

Chapter Two
ECONOMIC SYSTEMS

*Three Economic Questions—
A Traditional Economic System—
A Command Economic System—
The Market System—Mixed
Economic Systems*

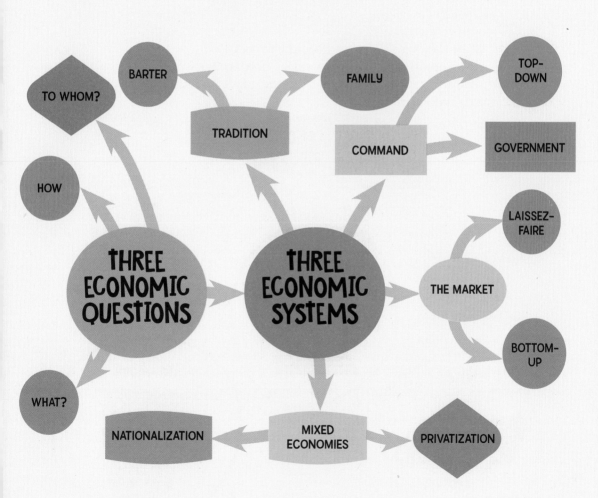

To solve the problem of scarcity, all economies have to answer three questions. Ranging from what we eat to how we work, our answers determine what we produce and who gets what. The answers come from three kinds of economic systems.

THREE ECONOMIC QUESTIONS

The answers to three questions determine what we produce and distribute. They decide the goods and services that individuals, households, businesses, and governments will receive, who will get more, and who will get less. Although they cover millions of people and countless goods and services, the questions are rather simple. They are:

1. What goods and services should be produced?
2. How should goods and services be produced?
3. Who will get the "income" from the goods and services that are produced?

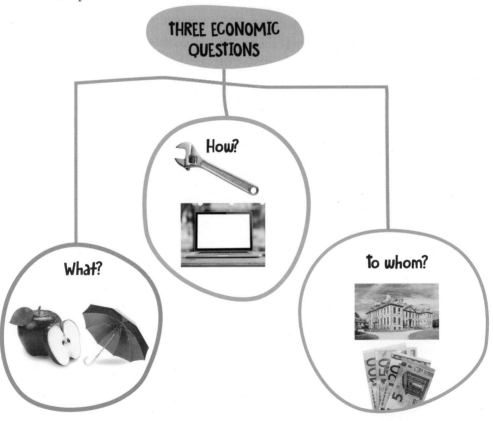

As you might expect, there are an unlimited number of answers. However, they all can be grouped within one of the three economic systems: tradition, command, and the market.

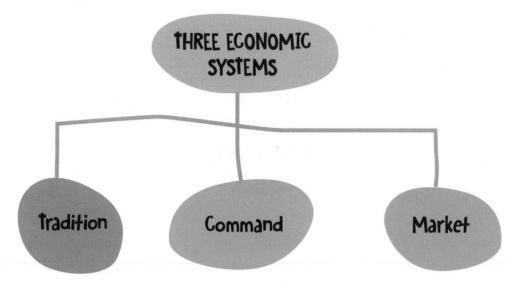

Traditional Economic System

With a traditional economic system, we would need a double coincidence of wants for most transactions. To get our latte, someone else has to want what we will offer—like some tea. Involving no money, the transaction is called barter:

TRADITION ▶ *an economic system that passes down from generation to generation the answers to the three economic questions.*

Command Economy

In a command economy, one person or group makes the economic decisions. To get our latte, the person or group in charge—usually the government—has to decide that it wants to use its land, labor, and capital to manufacture and sell coffee. With command, decisions move from the top down:

The Command Economic System

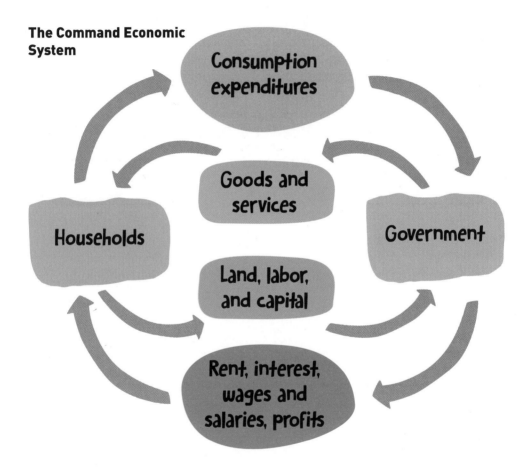

COMMAND ▶ *a top-down economic system through which one person or group of people answers the three economic questions.*

The Market

In a market system, millions of businesses decide what to produce. We are able to buy our latte because Starbucks and other coffee shops decided to sell it. The decisions for most of what consumers buy come from the bottom up:

The Market Economic System

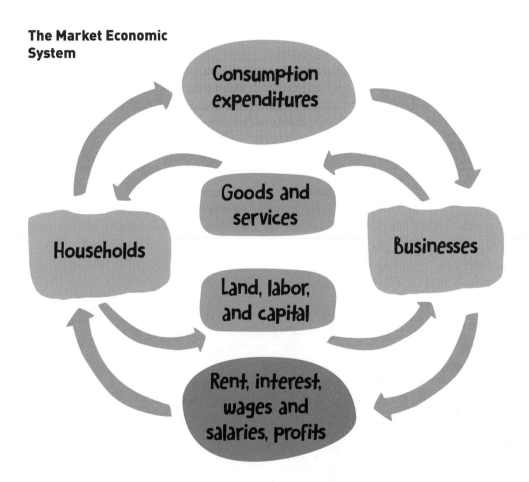

THE MARKET ▶ *a bottom-up economic system through which many people and businesses give the answers to the three economic questions by responding to supply-and-demand incentives.*

A TRADITIONAL ECONOMIC SYSTEM

Most simply described, a traditional economic system repeats the past. People know which goods and services to produce and how to distribute them because they have always done it the same way.

For a snapshot of a traditional economic system, we will take a look at the indigenous people called the Wampanoag that inhabited parts of the North Atlantic East Coast of the US several hundred years ago. Although relatively few Wampanoag remain, their traditional economic system is timeless. It is a system that, on the surface, appears uncomplicated. However, we will see that, for the Wampanoag and other traditional economies, there is much more. With knowledge of their fields, of the forest, and of the sea, they built homes and fed themselves. They constructed roadways, nourished the land, and had an interconnected network of summer and cold-weather residences. As a traditional economy, the knowledge that was passed from person to person focused on preserving the land and their community bonds.

Much about the Wampanoag is true for today's traditional economies. Although the picture is from the past, it still exists in groups that range from the Inuit of northern Canada to indigenous communities around India's Great Himalayan National Park.

The traditional economic system still exists in some groups of the Inuit who live in northern Canada.

The Wampanoag

Numbering as many as 24,000 people, in the early 17th century the Wampanoag lived in approximately 70 tribal communities. To convey an image of their traditional economic organization we can use some of the Wampanoag answers to "what, how, and to whom."

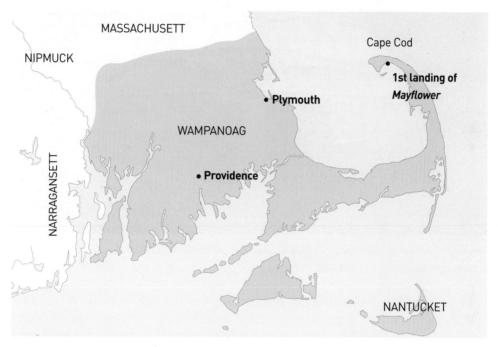

Location of the Wampanoag.

1. What do they produce?

When the English arrived in America on the *Mayflower* in November 1620, they saw evidence of a thriving civilization. All was deserted, though, because the Wampanoag had already moved inland for the winter.

In answer to the question of "what," the Wampanoag planted beans, corn, and squash in their fields; in the woods, they hunted deer and waterfowl, and gathered berries and nuts. In addition, near the coast, they collected clams, scallops, and crabs, and fished for sturgeon, haddock, cod, and other local seafood. We could add cranberries, lobsters, shark, and turtles to our "what" list and still it would not be complete. Their land and water were bountiful.

In another answer to "what," the Wampanoag built round houses called *wetus* framed with bent saplings in their multi-family villages. These homes

This wetu *is made from waterproof cattails. It would have housed one family group that included several generations during the spring and summer.*

were equipped with sleeping platforms that lined the inside walls. While their smaller summer dwellings accommodated an extended family group, the larger ones—as big as a football field—could have been used to house bigger groups or to host political events. Researchers have also uncovered underground pits nearby that display evidence the Wampanoag stored dried corn in them for the winter.

2. How do they produce?
For everyday tasks, the Wampanoag division of labor was gender-based. As "keepers of life," the women planted crops and bore children. Meanwhile, defense and hunting were among the men's responsibilities. Thinking of land, labor, and capital, economists would say that tasks were labor intensive.

With tools that included digging sticks and clamshell hoes, the Wampanoag used herring to fertilize their corn plants and mortars and pestles for grinding the corn into meal. Researchers also recovered the fired clay ceramic containers Wampanoag women used for cooking and storage and the baskets with which they transported clams. During the winter, the women spent their time weaving.

Somewhat like the women, the men sought to control the environment that supplied their food. They burned the underbrush in the forest in order to create a habitat where the deer, beaver, wolves, and the other animals they hunted could thrive. To trap deer, large numbers of Wampanoag men cooperated in a communal hunt through which they formed an increasingly narrow "deer run." From the forest's large trees, they made dugout canoes called *mishoons*. As they were unworried about theft, they left these canoes on creek beds so that travelers could use them to cross rivers. We also know that they built boats that could hold as many as 40 men, used stone arrowheads with their bows, blanketed the forest with spring traps, and channeled the waters with weirs.

If we followed the Wampanoag's seasonal migrations, we would have seen the coastal homes where they lived until the harvest, their larger winter dwellings that were farther inland, and their springtime settlements close to the riverside fish runs. We would also have seen the bulrush mat technology they developed to retain the heat in their winter homes. If we followed their middlemen, we would have seen how they facilitated coastal trading that extended up to Maine and Nova Scotia.

Because sharing a harvest of beans was very different from distributing the parts of a deer, the Wampanoag economy had to accommodate seasonal change. Depending on where, when, and what provisions they had, they could pivot their response to the three basic economic questions. Still, though, it was tradition that had the answers.

3. Who gets the income?

Initially, the Wampanoag had been known as a matrilineal society in which control of the land was passed from mother to daughter. Women also controlled the household. It is even possible that, after marriage, a man moved in with his wife's family. In addition, legends tell of women's councils where decisions were made.

However, scholars speculate that after the European settlers arrived in the 17th century, male leaders called *sachem* began to lead the Wampanoag. As leaders, *sachems* received furs, fields, labor, and the prime parts of game animals in tribute from the local community.

More horizontal than vertical, a communal value system based on sharing and exchange anchored Wampanoag society. Among countless interactions, ranging from marriage to mourning, individuals became more influential through gift-giving; people who exhibited selfishness or jealousy were compared to witches. Fundamentally, the Wampanoag had a partnership with each other and with the land that nurtured them.

**Features of Traditional
Economic Systems**

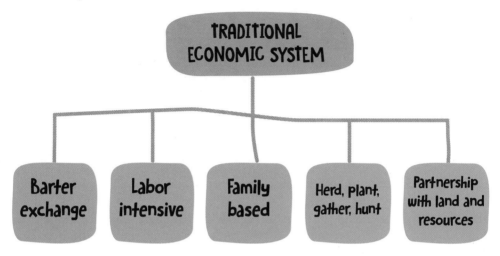

With the Europeans and the Wampanoag in the same place at the same time, the two groups traded and they fought. They supported and opposed each other. From the English, the Wampanoag received goods and power that elevated their position among other tribal groups. But, as the English population grew, the Wampanoag became an abused minority with less ability to maintain their traditions.

A COMMAND ECONOMIC SYSTEM

Moving from Massachusetts to Moscow, and from the 17th to the 20th century, we will see how tradition can become command. With "what, how, and to whom" decisions moving from the top downward, a Soviet command system replaced the traditional economy that begins our story in Russia.

The Osorgin Manor

Legend tells us that, in 1843, Mikhail Mikhailovich Osorgin was playing cards at an exclusive gentleman's club in Moscow when he heard someone at another table shout that his Kaluga estate was for sale for 600,000 rubles. "How happy I would be if a buyer showed up and freed me of it," he said. Without missing a beat, Mikhail Mikhailovich Osorgin bought it from him, there and then.

Located 90 miles (145 km) south of Moscow, the 8,327 acre (3,379 hectares) property remained in the Osorgin family for the next three generations. Encompassing forests, streams, and fields, their land included eight villages. The manor house was staffed with butlers, coachmen, cooks, and servants.

Until the Russian Revolution in 1917, for 75 occasionally tumultuous years, the family ran the estate. Whether looking at the Osorgins or the villagers, we would have seen tradition in operation throughout those decades. Villagers planted, hunted, and fished across yearly cycles that combined religion and economic activity. Even the amounts of mushrooms, nuts, and berries they harvested from the forests were constrained by the obligations between the Osorgins and their villagers that were passed down from generation to generation.

Mikhail Osorgin.

The Soviet Collective

All of this ended in 1918.

Confiscating the lands held by the wealthy, the Bolsheviks also nationalized the banks, levied new taxes, and temporarily gave land and homes to the peasants. Instead of tradition, the answers to "what, how, and to whom" now came from the government.

The Osorgin estate was nationalized when the Bolsheviks moved into the manor house and set up local communes. With their land, equipment, and animals taken from them, the family fled. Meanwhile, crushing any resistance in the province, the Bolsheviks established state farms, agricultural cooperatives, and agricultural associations.

Starting in 1928 with his first Five Year Plan, the Soviet leader Joseph Stalin collectivized the villages comprising the Osorgin Manor. This first Five Year Plan (which actually lasted 4½ years, from October 1, 1928 to December 31, 1932) created two kinds of agricultural units. *Sovkhozes* were agricultural factories with paid labor tilling the land. Somewhat different, a *kolkhoz* replaced the Osorgin Manor. On the farm and in the factory, planning committees decided who should produce, what, and how much.

NATIONALIZATION ▶ *the process through which the ownership of privately-owned property is transferred to the government.*

1. What do they produce?

Renamed Suvorov, the Osorgin Manor became a *kolkhoz* on which hundreds of peasant households produced crops, milk, and meat. Because the collectives were estimated to have received one-eighth of the market price, the remaining seven-eighths could be used for industrialization – in effect, these farmers subsidized the growth of industry.

Woefully unproductive, a *kolkhoz* harvested one-seventh (14.3 percent) of the grain that a British farm produced although it employed 10 times as many workers. While a Russian cow annually produced 650 gallons (2,955 liters) of milk, the average was 1,558 gallons (7,082 liters) in the United States. Even in the collective, a privately-owned cow produced 1,318 gallons (5,992 liters) of milk annually.

Demonstrating the power that a command economy can have, the country's first Five Year Plan successfully jump-started the transition from production that emphasized land and labor to a capital-intensive economy. By 1932, having built over 1,500 new factories, aviation, automobile manufacture, and electricity generation were just a few of the industries aside from agriculture that began to grow.

Cotton is weighed on a kolkhoz *in Uzbekistan.*

2. How do they produce?

A 1935 *kolkhoz* statute detailed its answers to "how." Through collectivization, the peasants worked the land together and cared for state-owned livestock. A field's boundaries were to be articulated in a document prepared by the District Executive Committee. Whether determined by local officials or higher-level planning committees, the *kolkhozniks* knew when and how to plant, plow, and sow. Including everything from irrigation to "timely and artful harvesting without losses," they were told their responsibilities at every stage of the agricultural process.

The *kolkhoz* documents also detailed what to do with the draught animals and the equipment (like harrows and threshers) the farm got from the local Machine Tractor Station. As for the labor, the collective's leader decided who did what.

The last ingredient in the "how" recipe was private plots. To assuage the anger of peasants who expected to have some of their own land to farm, each household was given a small plot and livestock that they had to pay for. The 1935 directive said, for example, that the households in one region in a particular kind of collective could own no more than one cow, two calves, one sow with its suckling, and not more than 10 sheep and 20 beehives. They could, however, keep an unlimited number of chickens and rabbits.

3. Who gets the income?

The collective knew that it had to allocate a proportion of its output for the group's social and cultural needs. They had to set aside funds for maintaining equipment, training, and treating illness. They also had to pay taxes and compensate the local Machine Tractor Station that assisted them. Whatever was left over went to the collective's members, based on the amount of work they did.

The most income came from the private plots. As a disproportionately large share of production, according to one estimate, in 1938, they represented 3.9 percent of all sown farmland and 45 percent of the output. They produced more than half of the country's potatoes, milk, and meat.

As economists, again we see the role of scarcity. During the second half of the 20th century, recognizing limited quantities of land, labor, and capital, Soviet planners answered our third question about income when they prioritized a space program and a powerful military. As a result, they had to minimize the production of consumer goods.

Returning to the location of the Osorgin Manor, they wound up with farmers receiving little return from what they collectively produced. They

Mikhail Gorbachev.

created a value system that condemned individual initiative, innovation, and private gain. Just picking up an abandoned potato from a field and selling it was prohibited.

Then, in 1991, everything changed again. A long list of factors, ranging from the United States' Cold War dominance to the Soviet leader Mikhail Gorbachev's policy of societal liberalization known as *glasnost* ("openness") have been named as reasons that the USSR dissolved. No longer dominated by Russia, the dissolution of the Soviet Union resulted in independence for 14 nations.

In Russia, they took the next step to a market economy. Through the economic reforms called *perestroika* ("restructuring") he introduced, Gorbachev had relaxed central control and let some farms and factories decide what to produce, what to charge, and even what profits they would make. Then, in 1991, by privatizing what had been state-owned enterprises, Russia moved farther away from a command economy.

On a local level, in December 1991 (the Soviet Union was formally dissolved on December 25, 1991), the Suvorov *kolkhoz* had to decide its future. At a meeting, its members were given three options. They could perpetuate the collective, with each member receiving ownership shares. More radically, they could allow the land to be divided and distributed as private plots. Finally, they were told the collective farm could be turned into a company owned by shareholders.

They selected the most familiar option and kept the collective. Although the new Russian leader Boris Yeltsin had untethered prices and was dismantling the command economy, the farmers of Suvorov retained the local version of "what, how, and to whom."

PRIVATIZATION ▶ *the process through which private individuals and businesses purchase state-owned enterprises.*

Like tradition, command is an economic system that is composed of much more than what we see on the surface. When a command economic system answers the three economic questions, planners have a gargantuan task. Among innumerable intermediate and final goods and services for consumers and industry, they have to decide what their land, labor, and capital will create. Imagine, for example, socks. Deciding how many you will produce of a final good like socks is only the beginning. Command economy committees also have to calculate what cotton to cultivate, how much fabric to make, and who might buy them. It was impossible for a planning committee to accurately predict an entire country's needs and wants.

Based on a cartoon in a satirical magazine: the perils of central planning. Because the plant manager was only given a weight quota to fulfil, he points with pride to a single massive nail.

Features of the Command Economic System

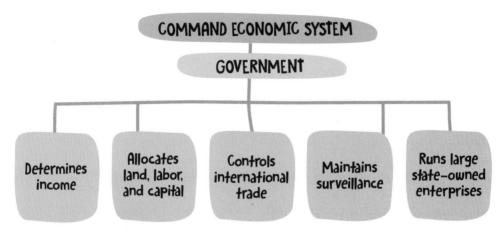

THE MARKET SYSTEM

Our third economic system takes us back to the United States. The place is New York, and the date is the early 19th century. Again, we start with a traditional economy. Soon, though, it becomes a market.

Thinking of the early 1800s, imagine a farm or an artisanal business. Most of the US population lived on farms, where home and work converged. Like most traditional economies, the women and men worked in the fields and also carried out gender-based tasks. Meanwhile, in towns and cities, the tailors, bakers, and printers stitched the clothing, made the bread, and published the newspapers.

There were a few factories, but they were not at that time the institutions that we might expect. In Rochester, New York, a factory would have had one room in which a group of 12 to 15 men gathered during the day. Overseen by a master, they processed the wheat from neighboring farms. Rather than money, it is more likely that they were paid with alcohol. In 1818, the city exported 26,000 barrels of wheat.

The Erie Canal

But then New York's Governor DeWitt Clinton proposed what had never been done before. He wanted to connect Albany and Buffalo, New York, with a canal (and Rochester was along the route). Before then, most canals in the US were fewer than 2 miles (3.2 km) long. If you had arranged them all in a single line, the US's entire canal network would have been just 100 miles (161 km) long.

DeWitt Clinton proposed a canal that would be an unheard-of 363 miles (585 km) long. To make it, the waterway's engineers would have to copy British technology. When they began in 1817, hydraulic cement had not yet been invented (it was developed the following year). They asked contractors to use their own tools and parceled out the construction work in small, multi-mile increments. Each segment, when completed, was opened for use.

It worked.

Completed in 1825, the Erie Canal transformed everything that it touched. Rochester's small factories soon needed to be relocated to larger buildings and with many more employees. By 1828, the city was exporting 220,000 barrels of processed wheat and was paying workers with money rather than alcohol. "Work" became the place where you gave your labor for 10 to 12 hours a day; "home" was where the women were.

Before the Erie Canal was dug, goods and people moved on country roads and rivers. After the canal, the economy accelerated. Instead of a 20-day wagon trip, the journey from New York City to Buffalo on water took six days.

Most crucially, though, the Canal showed that the whole of the western US could now be opened up. Copycat canals were built, and work on a

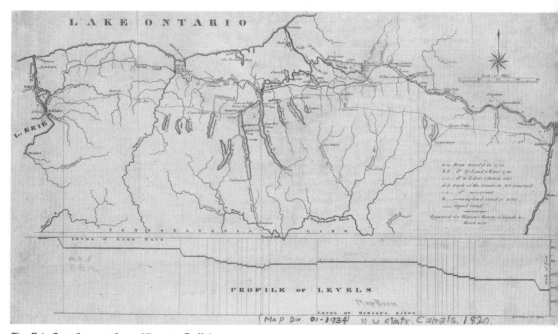

The Erie Canal's route from Albany to Buffalo.

"DOES NOT SUCH A MEETING MAKE AMENDS?"

A cartoon from 1869 celebrating the completion of the transcontinental railroad.

country-wide railroad network began. In 1869, the first transcontinental railroad was completed, when the existing eastern railroad network met Western railroads in Promontory Summit, Utah. At the same time, the telegraph made fast communication possible across vast distances. As these new forms of transport and communication "shrank" the vast distances and expanses of America, Congress responded by dividing the continent into four standardized time zones.

In 1815, hardly anyone at all in the US could afford to buy a mattress because they cost $50. In 1848, with regional specialization and the faster and cheaper movement of goods and resources making manufacturing more efficient, the price plunged to $5. By 1839, Rochester was exporting 500,000 barrels of processed wheat.

Rochester in 1860.

A National Market

As for "what, how, and to whom," by the middle of the 19th century the US had a market system that functioned from the bottom up. While no one told the country's manufacturers what to produce, the transport and communication system that developed ensured that people got what they needed and what they wanted. It did this in part by allowing businesses to specialize and trade more effectively. By now moving goods and people cheaply and speedily, the US economy was no longer dependent on self-contained regions. Instead, canals and then railroads enabled each region to do what it did best. The South could grow cotton and New England could make textiles. Meanwhile, farms in the West grew wheat and barley.

The "how" takes us to technology, starting with steam. Once it was possible to power boats, locomotives, and machinery with steam, economic activity was no longer limited mainly to the productivity of labor. The incentive behind these developments was "who gets the income." In a market system, profits push people to produce and distribute goods and services.

Features of the Market Economic System

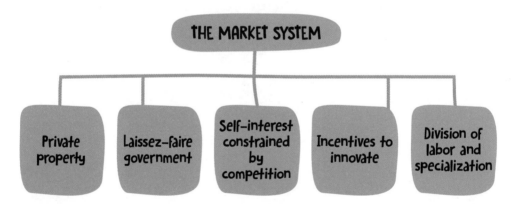

MIXED ECONOMIC SYSTEMS

At this point, you may have concluded that no economy is entirely traditional, centrally planned, or a market. And we can indeed mix and match all three. When the United States offered social security programs to its people, it added command to the market; the former Soviet Union's command system represented a glimmer of a viable market when farmers began to sell produce they had grown on their own land. Similarly, the economy of China today has been called a socialist market.

A Mixed Economic System

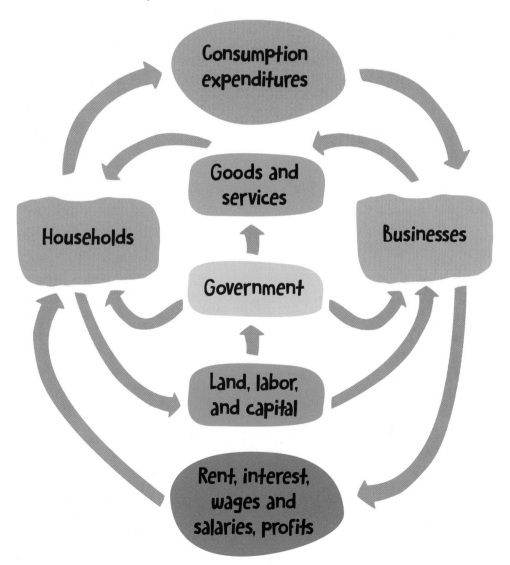

To see the world's economic systems, we can form a continuum with an entirely free market at one end and complete command at the other. Then, ranking the world's 178 countries, the Index of Economic Freedom positions Singapore and New Zealand in the top spots, with Venezuela and North Korea at the bottom. While they do not explicitly ask "what, how, and who," their criteria, including taxation, government size, rule of law, regulatory efficiency, and open markets, provide all the answers.

MIXED ECONOMY ▶ *an economic system that combines the characteristics of tradition, command, and/or the market.*

An Economic Systems Scale

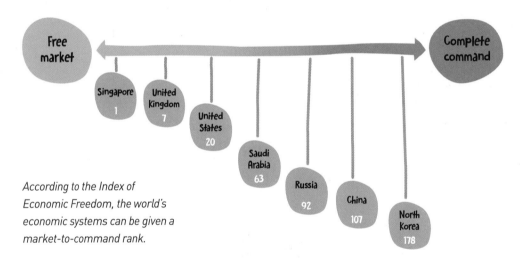

According to the Index of Economic Freedom, the world's economic systems can be given a market-to-command rank.

Free market

Singapore 1
United Kingdom 7
United States 20
Saudi Arabia 63
Russia 92
China 107
North Korea 178

Complete command

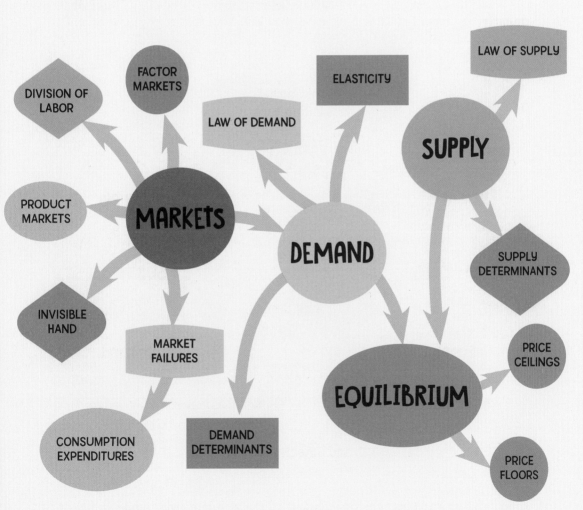

DIVISION OF LABOR

FACTOR MARKETS

LAW OF DEMAND

ELASTICITY

LAW OF SUPPLY

SUPPLY

PRODUCT MARKETS

MARKETS

DEMAND

SUPPLY DETERMINANTS

INVISIBLE HAND

MARKET FAILURES

EQUILIBRIUM

PRICE CEILINGS

CONSUMPTION EXPENDITURES

DEMAND DETERMINANTS

PRICE FLOORS

Moving on from all economic systems, our next step is the market. Whenever there's a price, there could be a market. Rather than a place, a market is a process that propels activity around our circular flow model as it determines how much we pay and what we produce. The market is where supply meets demand.

Returning to the Starbucks where we first entered the circular flow model, we stand in the line, place our order, and decide (maybe unknowingly) if the price is okay. The decision places us in a product market where we feel that $10 is too much and $2 too little. At $5, the amount sounds fine. Somewhat similarly, in factor markets, businesses and households determine what land, labor, and capital will cost.

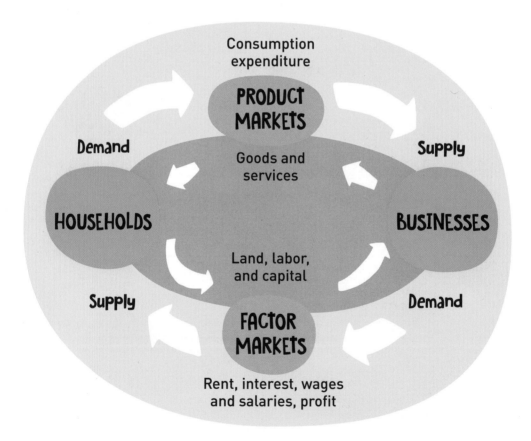

In product markets, households are on the demand side, while in factor markets they provide the supply.

FACTOR MARKETS ▶ *the markets in which the price and quantity of land, labor, and capital—the factors of production—are determined through supply and demand.*

PRODUCT MARKETS ▶ *the markets in which the price and quantity of goods and services are determined through supply and demand.*

MARKETS

In a market system, everywhere we look we see a market with a "sell" side and a "buy" side that create a price. A perfect example is your airline ticket. The number of buyers and unsold seats could have determined the price. Then, the airlines and their customers, each with their own incentives, decide if the price seems reasonable. The price conveys the information that businesses and consumers need before the sale.

Our task now is to look more closely at both sides of a market. We need to see how and why sellers decided what prices they prefer. Similarly, we will look more closely at what buyers are really thinking. While our example here is ice cream, it could be any good or service.

When buying an airline ticket, the price is determined by the number of buyers and the number of unsold seats.

PRICE ▶ *the main source of information from the market.*

SUPPLY

More than two decades before Unilever acquired Ben & Jerry's, they opened their first Scoop Shop in May 1978. While Ben and Jerry were not economists, they knew the right way to create supply.

Like all people that start a business, Ben and Jerry first had to work out the supply side of their venture. When economists refer to supply, they mean an entire schedule of price/quantity pairs. A schedule is the table of price quantity pairs on which you base your supply curve. Consequently, if you asked about the supply of ice cream, the answer would be a list of prices and quantities. For example, let's assume that when the price is 70 cents, they are able (using very simple hypothetical numbers) to produce 5 cones. However, at 60 cents, the total drops to 3.

Below, you can see a hypothetical supply schedule for ice cream cones for one day. As a supply schedule, it displays what an ice cream maker would be willing and able to produce at each price:

Price	Quantity
70 cents	5
65 cents	4
60 cents	3
55 cents	2
50 cents	1
45 cents	0

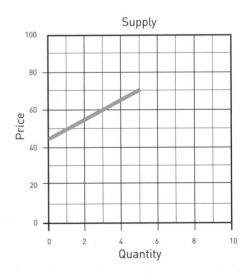

Naturally, as price rises, they are willing and able to make more. The basic reason is profit. Higher prices let them make more money.

> **SUPPLY** ▶ *the different price/quantity pairs at which a producer is willing and able to sell goods and services.*

Law of Supply

On the supply side, a schedule demonstrates the positive relationship between price and quantity. Called the law of supply, as price goes up, so too does the quantity supplied. Correspondingly, if price drops, quantity goes down. When you move from one price/quantity pair to another, you have a change in quantity supplied—not a change in supply.

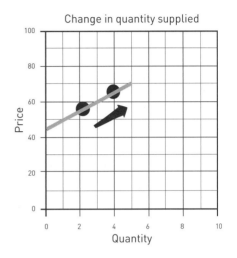

In the graph, moving from one dot to the other dot, after price went up, the quantity supplied moved from 2 to 4 ice cream cones. We can think of them as partners. When price rises, quantity follows.

Market Supply

So far, we have looked at a supply composed of one Scoop Shop; but of course, there is much more. To see the whole market's supply side, we multiply Column 1 by Column 2 to get Column 3:

Price ($)	Column 1 Individual supply Quantity supplied per single business	Column 2 Number of suppliers Number of sellers	Column 3 Market supply Total quantity supplied
70 cents	5	10	50
65 cents	4	10	40
60 cents	3	10	30
55 cents	2	10	20
50 cents	1	10	10
45 cents	0	10	0

Determinants of Supply

People who start businesses have to consider some supply basics. Those basics position their supply curve and move it when they change. They are called the determinants of supply.

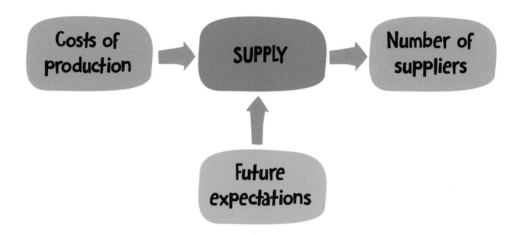

1. Cost of production:

The most important determinant of supply is the cost of production. Related to land, labor, and capital, changes in the cost of production can move the supply curve to the left or right. When the cost of production is higher, businesses are willing and able to make less, while lower costs have the opposite impact.

With little money and a small loan, Ben and Jerry kept production costs low. Unable to afford a renovation, they found a half-price walk-in freezer at an auction. Instead of new stainless-steel sinks, they complied with American health department regulations by bolting three fiberglass laundry containers together. Then, after opening, their costs went down because of a lucky accident. When a palette of candy bars fell off a shelf in their walk-in freezer, the chocolate crumbled ideally. Rather than cutting the chunks, they just needed a tall ladder. The new technology (the ladder) had reduced the cost of production.

Like Ben and Jerry, having little money to invest in the capital for an office or store, many people that start a business begin by using a garage, a church, or even a bathtub. In Bellevue, Washington, in 1994, Jeff Bezos stocked books and processed Amazon's first orders in his rented home's garage. In the late 1960s, Richard Branson ran one of his earliest ventures from an office in a church crypt in London. And, as a door-to-door fax-machine salesperson in Atlanta, Georgia, Sara Blakely came up with the idea for Spanx. Packing and shipping the products from her apartment, Blakely's bathtub doubled as her fulfillment center.

2. Future expectations:

Expectations also affect the position of the supply curve. For Ben and Jerry, it was seasonal. They knew they needed to produce less during the winter. When Sara Blakely got one of her first department store orders, she based her future expectations on the number of friends she was sure would buy her Spanx.

3. The number of suppliers:

Back in Burlington, Vermont, there were two other shops that sold ice cream. One was in the bus station. The other was a sandwich shop. Had other ice cream shops opened or closed in the city, it would have effected a change in market supply.

Initially, decisions that relate to the determinants of supply position a business's supply curve. Then, changes can move it. Displayed by Q2, it could have increased.

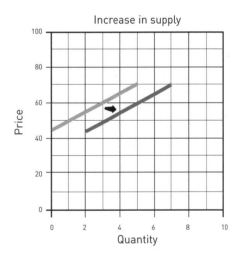

Increase in supply

Price ($)	Q1	Q2
70 cents	5	7
65 cents	4	6
60 cents	3	5
55 cents	2	4
50 cents	1	3
45 cents	0	2

DEMAND

Like supply, demand is the entire schedule of price/quantity pairs. For a family, during one day, the demand for ice cream cones could be 1 if the price was 65 cents, 2 if it went down to 60 cents, and 5 for a 45-cent bargain. On an entire hypothetical demand schedule for ice cream cones, we can record what consumers are willing and able to buy at each price.

Price ($)	Quantity
70 cents	0
65 cents	1
60 cents	2
55 cents	3
50 cents	4
45 cents	5

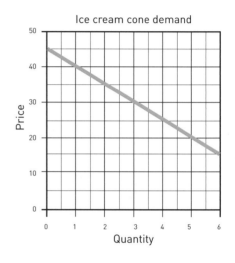

Ice cream cone demand

Law of Demand

As you can see, the demand schedule demonstrates the inverse relationship between price and quantity. Called the law of demand, as price goes up, the quantity demanded goes down. Correspondingly, when price descends, quantity rises. So, when you move from one price/quantity pair to another, you have a change in quantity demanded.

Ben & Jerry's big promotion was POPCDBZWE (Penny Off Per Celsius Degree Below Zero Winter Extravaganza). As price (and temperature) went down, the goal was an increase in the quantity demanded.

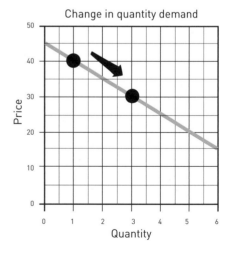

Change in quantity demand

Market Demand

Like the supply side, we can move from individual demand to the entire market. To see the demand side of the whole market, we just multiply Column 1 by Column 2 to get Column 3:

Price ($)	Column 1 Individual demand — Quantity demanded per single business	Column 2 Buyers' quantity demanded — Number of buyers	Column 3 Market demand — Total quantity demand
70 cents	0	10	0
65 cents	1	10	10
60 cents	2	10	20
55 cents	3	10	30
50 cents	4	10	40
45 cents	5	10	50

DEMAND ▶ *the price and quantity at which the quantity supplied and the quantity demanded are equal.*

Demand Determinants

It is also possible for demand to increase or decrease. To see why, we can look at the determinants of demand.

NORMAL GOODS ▶ *the goods and services that we are willing and able to purchase more of when our income rises and less when it falls. Most everyday items are normal goods and services.*

INFERIOR GOODS ▶ *the lower quality goods and services that we are willing and able to purchase less of when our income rises and more of when it falls.*

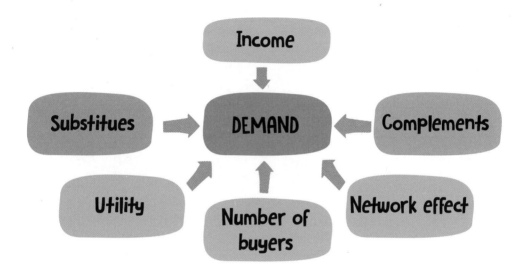

1. Income

If your income increases then your demand will go up. Earning more, you no longer need to buy less tasty ice cream. Instead, your demand soars for Ben & Jerry's or Häagen-Dazs or other premium ice creams. You could also buy more books from Amazon or an extra pair of Spanx. An economist would say your demand for normal goods went up because of an income increase.

Correspondingly, earning less brings demand down. The one exception is low quality. With a decrease in income, you have the incentive to buy fewer normal goods and more of those that are inferior.

2. Substitutes

A change in quantity demanded or a change in demand for one item can change our demand for something else. It could be frozen yogurt prices influencing ice cream purchases, cheaper socks changing Spanx demand, or digital books affecting people's propensity for buying physical books. Whatever the substitute, demand would respond with more or less.

3. Complements

Peanut butter and jelly are always the perfect example of complementary products. A change in one—perhaps its price or utility—could affect the demand for the other item. Buying a razor, we need razor blades. For my flashlight, I need batteries. Like peanut butter and jelly, the two go together. More of one makes you want more of the other. And yes, the opposite is also true. A less attractive or more expensive complement brings demand down for the other item.

A flashlight and batteries are an example of complementary products. If you buy the former, you will need to buy more of the latter.

4. Utility

Remembering that utility is usefulness or satisfaction, the utility of ice cream plunges when we learn that ice cream consumption causes more heart disease. Or, we want more sweaters in newly trendy colors. For either reason and countless others, more or less utility will change our demand for the goods and services we are willing and able to buy.

5. Number of Buyers

Predictably, the size of a market affects the position of the demand curve. For ice cream, it could be the weather; with clothing it is new styles. For Amazon, it was Prime. With each, we have changes in the size of the market affecting the position of the demand curve.

6. The Network Effect

Perhaps more closely related to social media than ice cream or Amazon, the creation of a network builds demand in an entire market. More participants lead to more participants.

Shown on the schedule below, when demand increases for ice cream, the curve shifts to the right:

Price ($)	Q1	Q2
75 cents	0	1
70 cents	0	2
65 cents	1	3
60 cents	2	4
55 cents	3	5
50 cents	4	6
45 cents	5	7

Price Elasticity: Elastic and Inelastic Demand

Demand curves also illustrate how much or how little consumers care about price changes. Called elasticity, we just have to imagine the quantity we demand as a rubber band that stretches or contracts when price changes. If price descends by a relatively small amount and the quantity demanded goes up by a lot, then we have elastic demand. However, if the response is minimal, an economist would say there was an inelasticity of demand.

As you might expect, items with many substitutes have elastic demand, as do luxuries. With each one, if the price goes too high, we can change to something else or postpone a purchase. However, for a necessity such as medication or milk, even a big jump in price will not persuade us to forgo the purchase. We tend to have inelastic demand for what we really need.

The formula for calculating the price elasticity of demand is below. If the answer is less than one, we have inelasticity; more than one means the item is elastic. Working out an answer, we can ignore whether the number is positive or negative.

$$\frac{\% \text{ change in quantity demanded}}{\% \text{ change in price}}$$

ELASTICITY ▶ *the extent to which a change in price affects a change in quantity demanded.*

EQUILIBRIUM

At this point, we need to imagine a room with two separate groups of people. On one side, we have supply where producers want the profits that higher prices can create. Facing them, on the demand side, individuals and businesses respond favorably to lower prices. For demand and supply, the determinants position the curves and shift them.

The price and quantity at which the supply and demand curves cross is called equilibrium. Because the quantities supplied and demanded are equal, it's called the market-clearing price. It is the price toward which markets move.

Let's assume (using very unrealistic but easy numbers), for example, that Ben and Jerry had misjudged their customers and charged too much. At 60 cents they would have finished with a surplus. They had 3 cones but customers only wanted 2. The next day, to compensate, maybe they lowered the price too much. Finally, on the third day, avoiding a surplus and a shortage, they got it right and charged a 55 cent equilibrium price. (They really did charge 55 cents for a cone in 1978. By 2022, in New York City, a small cone was $5.23) As a result, the quantity supplied is equal to the quantity demanded.

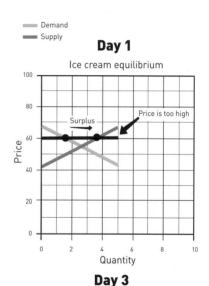

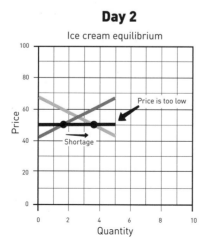

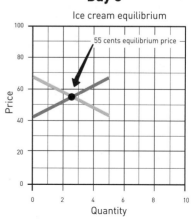

Price naturally moves to a level that is neither too high nor too low. It moves to an equilibrium where it is "just right."

EQUILIBRIUM ▶ *the price and quantity at which the quantity supplied and the quantity demanded are equal.*

MARKET FAILURE

Sometimes, however, supply and demand create an equilibrium price that is too high or too low. Then we can say that the market has failed. The classic example for too low a price is a manufacturing plant that causes pollution. During 2013, for example, people living close to the hot sauce maker Sriracha's factory complained that the spicy aromas emanating from it were giving them watery eyes and headaches. The aroma is the result of the close to 50,000 tons (45,360 tonnes) of chilis the factory processes during the fall. If indeed Sriracha's chilis were causing the neighbors' maladies (it is unclear), economists would call the phenomenon a market failure because it created a negative externality—a harmful impact on individuals that is beyond and unrelated to its source.

The Sriracha factory at Irwindale, California.

MARKET FAILURE ▶ *when the market's equilibrium price inadequately reflects the cost of societal cost or benefit.*

A negative externality reflects an equilibrium price that is too low. If the cost to Sriracha's neighbors was included, then we would have less supply. You can see on the negative externality graph that a supply curve that reflects a higher production cost encourages the producer to make less:

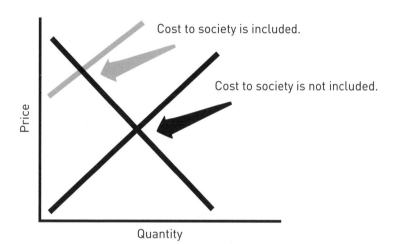

Cost to society is included.

Cost to society is not included.

Price

Quantity

The British economist Arthur Pigou had a solution to negative externalities. The Pigovian remedy was a "win/win" tax, so called because the money paid by the polluter goes to the municipality. As a result, supply decreases because of the expense the pollutant incurs or the community benefits from the extra revenue.

Arthur Pigou.

As you might expect, we can also have positive externalities when the market price inaccurately reflects the benefits of a transaction beyond the two parties involved. With vaccines, for example, an inoculated person prevents far more people from getting ill than just herself. As a result, the demand curve should have been placed to the right of its current location.

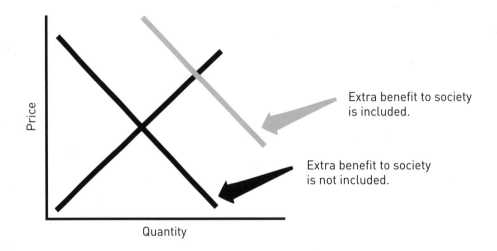

Extra benefit to society is included.

Extra benefit to society is not included.

EXTERNALITY ▶ *the positive or negative impact of a contract or decision as it ripples beyond its original source.*

PRICE CEILINGS AND FLOORS
Sometimes, even when the market accurately does its job, government still steps in to change the outcome by imposing a ceiling or a floor.

Price Floors
The most typical example of a price floor is the minimum wage. This is most commonly the lowest amount a person can receive for their labor, per hour. For example, several municipalities in the US in 2022 set their minimum wage around $15; in the UK, it was £9.50. On a minimum wage graph, the supply

curve represents the workers and demand comes from the employers. The horizontal line above equilibrium is the minimum wage.

PRICE FLOOR ▶ *typically mandated by government, a price for a good or service that is above equilibrium.*

Price floors may be implemented, as with the minimum wage, to ensure that the producers receive a fair price. But they can also be used to change behavior. In 2018, Scotland established a minimum price for alcohol with the aim of generating a decrease in sales (which did fall by almost 8 percent).

Located above equilibrium on a graph, floors illustrate surpluses. (The floor is above equilibrium because it stops us from going down any further.) While the message from the graph is to worry about a surplus, in real life there might not even be one. Too many other variables can affect the outcome.

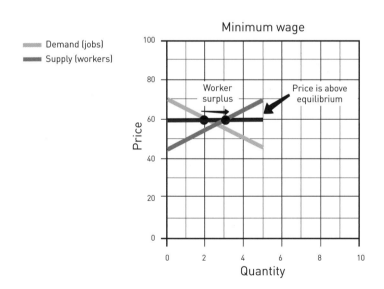

Price Ceilings

Similar to a floor, but its mirror image, a ceiling prevents prices from moving up to equilibrium. Because a ceiling is below equilibrium, it intersects with a higher quantity demanded than supplied. As a result, we wind up with a shortage.

> **PRICE CEILING** ▶ *typically mandated by government, a price for a good or service that is below equilibrium.*

The most typical price ceiling is rent control. To create more affordable housing, lawmakers proclaim a ceiling that prevents rents from rising in certain buildings. Predictably, landlords don't like rent control.

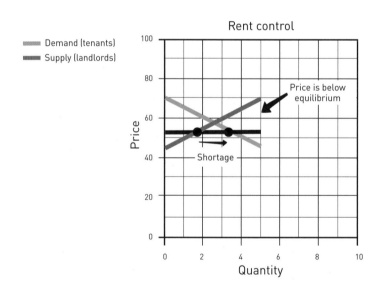

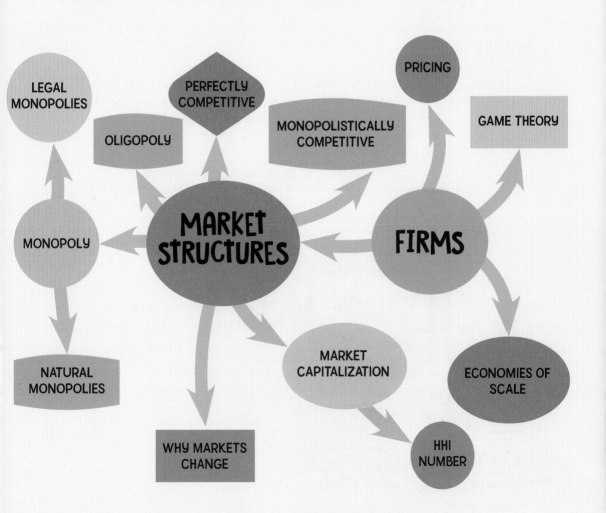

Millions of businesses make our supply decisions. Looking closely, we can see that each business behaves somewhat differently. It all depends on its market. Just like the light bulb and the automobile, the business is an invention.

Functioning somewhat like people, corporations sign contracts, make things, pay incomes, and organize land, labor, and capital into productive configurations. While there are many forms of businesses, such as partnerships and sole proprietorships, it is corporations that will be the main focus in the pages that follow. In the world of business, it is corporations that have attracted the most investors and thrived, in large part because they can limit their owners' liability.

TWO APPLES

We can start with two apples.

The first apple takes us to Sunnyvale, California, in the early 1970s. Steve Jobs and Steve Wozniak were friends who enjoyed playing around with electronics. As a teen, Wozniak won science prizes for creating gadgets like his electronic tic-tac-toe device. At the same time, Jobs was making his own inventions, experimenting, and visiting local tech laboratories. After high school, separately and together they attended and left college, designed video games, and traveled. In 1976, they decided to start their own company in an industry that did not yet really exist. The first question was what to name their new venture. They narrowed it down to Executek, Matrix Electronics, or Apple.

The rest is history.

An Apple Mac from 1984.

The second apple was developed at the University of Minnesota in the 1980s. At the time, most American apples were pretty much the same, with the selection typically limited to Red Delicious, Golden Delicious, or McIntosh. Elevating the taste of an apple to new sweet and crunchy highs, the Honeycrisp found its home on any farm that was willing to pay its developers. Like any innovation, the Honeycrisp was subject to research, development, and the request for a patent.

What Businesses Produce

Although vastly different, the Apple Computer and the Honeycrisp apple were similar because both needed a business to achieve success. Oases of command in the middle of the market, businesses are typically run from the top down. While businesses produce goods and services, statisticians include other categories such as construction.

Large and small, a majority of the 25.9 million active establishments in the EU produced services in 2019. Services that ranged from financial advice to yoga lessons and dental examinations dominated the business landscape in the US and UK in the same period.

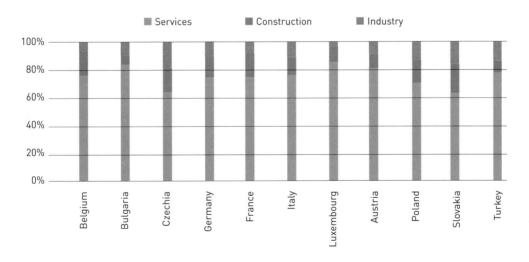

Among the 25.9 million businesses in the EU, the vast majority produce services.

Like the market system, composed of so many millions of establishments, the business sector can appear chaotic. However, just by looking at a scale along which business behavior can be grouped, we can achieve order and some insight.

FOUR COMPETITIVE MARKET STRUCTURES

Your local supermarket would never pay millions for a World Cup advertisement, but Barclays, Samsung, and Coca-Cola did. The reason why is the market in which each one competes.

Remembering that a market is a process that determines price and quantity, we now need to see how, depending on the market, price and quantity vary. Some competitive markets are populated by large firms while others are small. In some markets, businesses have control over prices, while in others, they don't.

We can say that there are four competitive market structures:
- perfect competition
- monopolistic competition
- oligopoly
- monopoly.

But not really.

Because firms occupy a market structure scale that displays increasing power, there are many more than four slots. The two extremes are perfect competition and monopoly. Then, in the middle we have monopolistic competition and oligopoly. The firm's market power determines its position on the scale. As a result, asked to name a random list of businesses, you could select a local barber, a Tesco supermarket, Kellogg's cereal, Spotify, and Microsoft. Along a market structure scale, the barber would come first and then the supermarket. Moving to the right, you then would have Kellogg's cereal, Spotify, and Microsoft.

As you can see, the order is related to the size and power of the firm. We care about its position on the scale because a firm's market structure shapes its behavior.

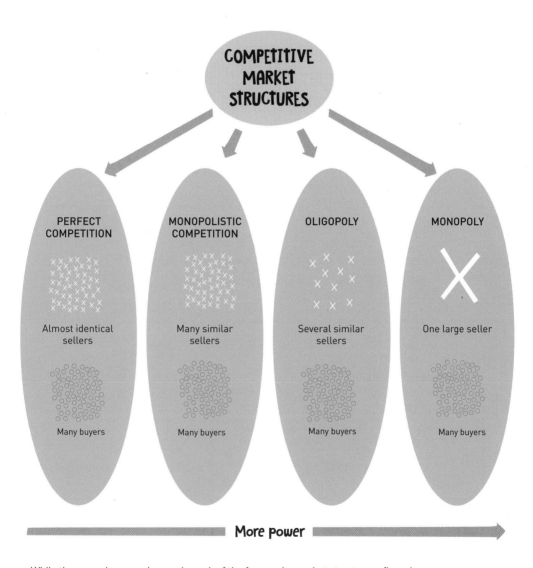

While there can be many buyers in each of the four main market structures, firm size grows as you approach the right margin. Moving to the right on a scale displaying the four basic competitive market structures, we see firms' market power increase.

> **COMPETITIVE MARKET STRUCTURES** ▶ *the markets in which businesses compete that are each characterized by more or less power for the firm.*

PERFECTLY COMPETITIVE FIRMS

To see a perfectly competitive business, we can return to our apple. It could be a Red Delicious or a McIntosh.

When you go into a supermarket you do not have a clue who grew the apple you select from a huge bin. Your apple looks like all of the other apples and tastes like them too.

In a perfectly competitive market, firms are small and their products are almost identical. For that reason, apple farmers have little power. They have no need to advertise. Furthermore, if they try to increase their price, they lose business. Similarly, there is no point in charging less because the market has made sure that everyone has produced their apples in the most efficient way. If a farmer tries to charge less, she loses money.

As a result, the farmer's market is the boss. Composed of many firms and many buyers, it tells her what to charge:

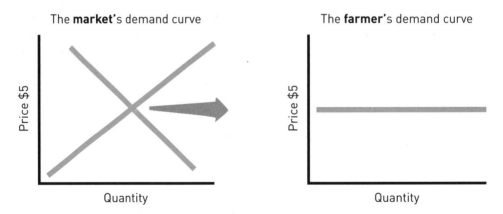

Through market supply and demand, farmers' prices are determined.

Summary

For the characteristics of perfect competition, we can say that there are many small firms that we can call price takers with almost identical products. Able to enter and leave the market easily, their behavior responds to the incentives created by the market's supply and demand.

> **PERFECT COMPETITION ▶** *a market composed of many firms and many consumers. Firms engaging in markets that resemble perfect competition are small, they are price takers, their products are almost identical, and they can enter the market relatively easily.*

MONOPOLISTICALLY COMPETITIVE FIRMS

When the University of Minnesota patented its Honeycrisp, it moved its apple to the right on a market structure scale from perfect competition to monopolistic competition. No longer the same as other apples, it has a name and a higher price. To some extent the Honeycrisp competes against other apples. But the "monopolistic" half of its monopolistic competition market structure name implies something unique about the product. As a result, the apple acquired an identity that separated it from all other apples. It gave the farmer a degree of pricing power.

There is a long list of firms in the monopolistically competitive region on the scale. They range from your small local barbershop where market entry is easy to a Starbucks cafe and a large chain of supermarkets. For each of these firms, they are like all of the others in the same business.

BUT...

Each one also has something unique that earns it partial "monopoly" status. If you were deposited in a Dunkin' Donuts you would know you were not in a Starbucks. If the name of the supermarket was covered up when you walked in, you would still be able to recognize it as a Carrefour, an Aldi, or a Walmart.

Summary

For monopolistic competition, we have many small- to medium-sized businesses. Their pricing power can depend on their uniqueness. Market entry and exit also vary but can be rather simple. If you want to start a local barbershop, you won't need huge funding to enter the business.

MONOPOLISTIC COMPETITION ▶ *a market composed of many firms and many consumers. Firms engaging in monopolistic competition range from small to somewhat large, and they have some pricing power, their products are similar and yet unique, and they can enter and exit the market relatively easily.*

OLIGOPOLY

Oligopolies are located further to the right along a market structure scale. They include very large firms, many of which have a global reach, such as Apple, automobile manufacturers, and the drinks makers that can distinguish themselves from the other producers that make the same products. There are though some oligopolies, like steelmakers, that have the same products.

All of these businesses seek the product differentiation that gives them more market power. For Coke and Pepsi, one difference is taste. With steel-makers, whose steel might be the same, they could use customer service or delivery times to distinguish themselves from everyone else.

Coke and Pepsi use product differentiation to give themselves more market power.

Because they have many consumers, oligopolies can mass produce their goods. Frequently, mass production facilitates an economy of scale through which each additional item's cost is less. Because the land, labor, and capital required to achieve an economy of scale can be considerable, they require the bigger businesses that can afford large production facilities. From there, those firms also need the advertising that connects them to many consumers. They use global supply chains that link the makers of their product's components. Your LEGO could have been produced from plastic made from Saudi Arabian oil while its actual manufacture took place in Denmark.

Meanwhile, oligopoly behavior could be based on game theory, when a production decision relates to what you expect your competitor will do. Called the prisoner's dilemma, it uses the example of two prisoners' desire to minimize their time in jail. With the two prisoners separated after their arrest, they have to guess which of several scenarios will optimize their own individual outcome. Their options are summarized in this table:

| | | PRISONER B | |
		Remain silent	Confess
PRISONER A	Remain silent	A gets 5 years. B gets 5 years.	A gets 10 years. B gets 1 year.
	Confess	A gets 1 year. B gets 10 years.	A gets 8 years. B gets 8 years.

An oligopoly contemplating a product roll-out can face the same dilemma as the prisoners. Somewhat similar to the prisoners, they cannot share information (because competition, or antitrust, laws in the EU, UK, and US, for example, prohibit collusion).

Oligopolies face the prisoner's dilemma when deciding whether to cut prices. It is also relevant for a number of other decisions in an oligopoly: when carmakers must decide how fast to produce an all-electric model, or when H&M plans the number of new lines it will introduce.

Summary

For oligopoly, we have few firms, many consumers, and product differentiation. Furthermore, while size and expense make entry and exit rather difficult, it creates businesses that are price makers rather than price takers.

At this point, we should note that the internet creates exceptions. At the margin, smaller internet companies experience little extra cost to produce massive quantities of services. Unlike traditional oligopolies, they have easy entry and exit and a large number of consumers.

> **OLIGOPOLY** ▶ *a market composed of few firms and many consumers. Firms in oligopolistic markets are quite large, and, as price makers, they have pricing power, their products can be differentiated or similar, and market entry and exit are difficult.*

MONOPOLY

Finally, we have monopoly. As a market structure with one firm, monopoly represents the pinnacle of power. Still, though, consumers have some say. There is a point as price ascends where their demand becomes elastic and they decide to stop buying. Also, there comes a point when government steps in and prohibits so large a firm from existing. While monopolies are usually large firms that have a global or national reach, it is also possible to have a single town or locality's smaller entity with monopoly power: the one physician in a village has a monopoly, as does the single newspaper.

> **MONOPOLY** ▶ *a market composed of one firm and many consumers. Monopolies are usually quite large, and, as price makers, they have considerable pricing power. It is almost impossible to enter a market dominated by a monopoly. Not to be confused with monopsony, which is a market in which there is one buyer.*

Natural and Legal Monopolies

Sometimes, though, it makes sense for government to allow a monopoly to exist. Called natural monopolies, some large firms help us avoid duplication. They could be a water company whose pipes service a town, for example. In situations such as this, it is wasteful to have several companies providing a service that one company could supply more efficiently.

The EU makes monopolies legal when it bestows a protected designation on a product. Champagne can only be labeled and sold as such if it comes from the Champagne region in France; Parma ham must be made in Parma, in Italy. For the UK, Brexit changed the market structure in which West County Cheddar Cheese competes. When the UK left the EU's single market in 2020 it moved the cheese to the left on the competitive market structure scale—perhaps to monopolistic competition. No longer protected, firms that make the cheddar will probably behave differently—rivals may begin branding their cheese as "cheddar" for example.

Champagne can only be produced in the Champagne region of France—it is a legal monopoly.

NATURAL MONOPOLY ▶ *a monopoly that lets the market avoid wasteful duplication and thereby is viewed somewhat favorably.*

Market Concentration

It also would change the concentration ratio of the market in which the West County Cheddar Cheesemakers compete. With concentration defined as the extent to which a specific number of firms (typically ranging from two to eight) dominate economic activity we can hypothesize the market structure. The simplest way is to add up market shares. For carbonated soft drinks in the US in 2021, Coca-Cola had a 46.3 percent market share, PepsiCo was at 25.6 percent, and Keurig Dr. Pepper, 21.7 percent. At a three firm concentration ratio of 93.6, the soft drink industry is well above 60, the dividing line between more competitive markets and oligopoly.

The Herfindahl-Hirschman Index (HHI) number is considered a more accurate means of discovering an industry's concentration ratio. To calculate it, you square the market share of each firm in the market and then add them together. Inversely related, fewer firms create a higher HHI number. Markets with an index number of 1,500 to 2,500 are moderately concentrated, and those with a number above 2,500 are highly concentrated, less competitive markets. HHI can be used to gauge the impact of an acquisition or merger. When it rises by 200, government alarm bells begin to sound.

Summary

In this final summary, we can say that a monopoly is a market with a single firm that is usually rather large. As a price maker, it has pricing power and many consumers.

Graphs

Using graphs, we can distinguish the different market structures by seeing how their characteristics change for the individual firm as we move to the right towards monopoly. We start with the horizontal line faced by the perfectly competitive firm. Then, though, reflecting some pricing power and the consumer response, demand curves begin to slope downward.

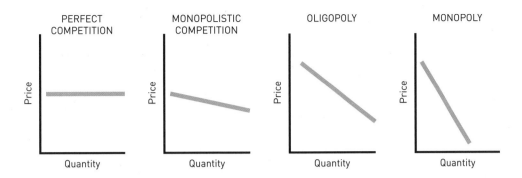

A firm's demand curve in different market structures.

Depending on your market structure, costs curves also differ.

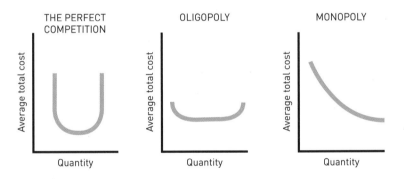

Although an immense oversimplification, the above costs still accurately display how larger firms take advantage of the economies of scale.

ECONOMIES OF SCALE ▶ *the lower cost per item that large firms enjoy when they produce large quantities of goods.*

Market Structure Characteristics

	Firm size	Pricing power	Number of firms	Product differentiation	Ease of market entry and exit	Price taker or maker
Perfect competition	Small	None	Very many	Minimal	Easy	Price taker
Monopolistic competition	Varies from small to large	Some	Many	Same and different	Somewhat easy	Price taker and maker
Oligopoly	Large	A lot	A few	Differentiated & undifferentiated	Difficult	Price maker
Monopoly	Usually very large	N/A	One	One firm	Very difficult	Price maker

HOW COMPETITIVE MARKET STRUCTURES CHANGE

Less Government Regulation: Southwest Airlines

Before 1978, the Civil Aeronautics Board (CAB) had always told airlines what they could and could not do in the US. As the federal regulator for all interstate flights, the CAB set fares, allocated routes, and limited market entry. For the larger carriers, it must have been somewhat pleasant. Their fares were high, inefficiency was okay, and returns were guaranteed. Carriers competed with each other to provide the best meals and service. One New York to Washington shuttle service even guaranteed its customers a seat by keeping an extra plane in reserve if needed.

In Texas, two men had a better idea. Knowing that intrastate airlines were outside the CAB's reach, Rollin King and Herb Kelleher started a low fare, high frequency airline and called it Southwest. At first connecting Houston, Dallas, and San Antonio, within six years Southwest was serving up to 10 cities. Flights had grown by 418 percent and passenger numbers by 1,042 percent. Challenging Southwest's formula and even its right to exist, the bigger carriers repeatedly took it to court and lost. Southwest's expansion, however, was limited to Texas. If it had tried to operate flights elsewhere, it would have been subject to CAB rules and regulations.

But then, with the Airline Deregulation Act of 1978, Congress changed the industry's market structure. No longer establishing fares, routes, and market entry and exit, the federal government's main responsibility was safety. In response, Southwest moved beyond its Texas borders. It had a distinctive culture with funny flight attendants. By flying on 737s and no other kind of planes, they were able to speed up their cleanup and maintenance procedures and turn their flights around quickly. It flew point-to-point, whereas other airlines operated from a hub-and-spoke network, and used smaller, less expensive airports.

Nudging fares lower and traffic higher, the "Southwest effect" took the airline industry to the left along our competitive market structure scale. The new market structure changed behavior, with Southwest leading the way and pulling others along with it. By increasing competition, the Southwest effect injected a dose of market efficiency.

Southwest Airlines.

Global airline market share, revenue, 2019

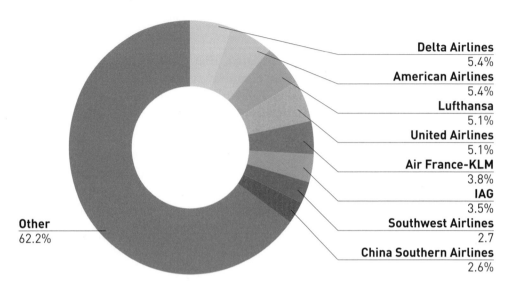

Delta Airlines
5.4%
American Airlines
5.4%
Lufthansa
5.1%
United Airlines
5.1%
Air France-KLM
3.8%
IAG
3.5%
Southwest Airlines
2.7
China Southern Airlines
2.6%

Other
62.2%

Deregulation made it easier for US airlines to compete globally. Because of deregulation, airlines responded to new incentives. Decades later, the new market encouraged airlines to downsize food portions and also seat sizes and leg room.

More Government Regulation: Microsoft Corporation

In 1968, when laptops did not exist, using a computer meant operating a mainframe. So, when a seventh-grade student at a private school in Seattle, Washington, wanted computer time, he had to pay for the hours on a teletype device that fed the data to an offsite mainframe computer.

With his friend Paul Allen, Bill Gates instructed the equipment to play games. They also worked out how to violate the computer's security system and were able to reduce their time records so that they owed less. Seeing their talent, the computer company hired them to fix the bugs they uncovered. Meanwhile, their own school prohibited them from using the computer for six weeks.

After high school, Bill Gates left Harvard (twice) without graduating. Instead, he and Allen started a company that they called Microsoft (Micro for small, soft for software). At the time, in 1975, personal computers (PCs) were rare. The Altair was the most commonly used PC, and was essentially a circuit board and some wires. Users would assemble their Altair and then decide what to do with it. One of its more popular applications was that it allowed its operator to control a robot by flipping a series of toggle switches.

Gates and Allen, though, were convinced they could make personal computers that were more useful. They just needed to write a language that it could follow.

The Altair 8800 from 1975.

And they did.

Their one especially lucrative product was their Microsoft Disk Operating System (MS-DOS). When IBM released their first PC in 1981 it used the MS-DOS operating system. It quickly became the go-to operating system for PCs (Apple, which began making home-use computers in the mid-1970s, developed its own proprietary operating system and the computer market was split between PC and "Mac" users). Even though Apple's macOS operating system was technically a rival to Microsoft's MS-DOS, Apple's share of the computer market was so small (around 4–6 percent in its earliest days) that Gates and Allen had the field almost to themselves. MS-DOS came preinstalled on all of IBM's PCs—and Gates and Allen retained the rights to every piece of their software running every IBM PC. As new computer manufacturers joined the PC market, they too used Microsoft's operating systems, which were upgraded every few years: Windows 3.0 in 1990, Windows 95 in 1995, Windows 98 in 1998, and so on. As well as operating systems, Microsoft developed other software such as the Office suite that included word processing and spreadsheet programs. They also created the Internet Explorer (IE) web browser. This meant that any person buying and using a PC (and not a Mac) was virtually guaranteed to be using at least one Microsoft product.

Microsoft's software was so successful that it left little room for competitors.

In May 1998, the US government and 20 separate American states brought charges against Microsoft for illegal restraint of trade. Their argument was that Microsoft's Windows operating system made it difficult, if not impossible, for buyers to augment their PCs with certain types of alternative software. The case against Microsoft centered around its IE web browser. As it was part of the MS-DOS operating system and came preinstalled on PCs, those who wished to use other browsers, such as the popular Netscape Navigator, were often unable to do so.

This is a situation that takes us straight to market structure. The suit against Microsoft claimed that the company was exerting monopoly power because it was offered as the only option on many new computers. Furthermore, any competitor's market entry was made even more difficult because of a network effect that encouraged programmers to develop applications that were compatible with Windows. Bundled into Windows' operating system package, IE precluded other browsers from competing in the market.

Responding to the government's challenge, Microsoft asserted that constraining them would harm innovation and product development. It could prevent them from competing globally and harm consumers, they claimed.

However, the courts decided that Microsoft was in violation of sections of America's antitrust law and ordered that the company be divided into two "Baby Bills": with one business responsible for operating systems and the other concerned exclusively with software development. Microsoft appealed against the ruling and, eventually, it was mandated that Microsoft could remain intact but had to open up its operating systems so that non-Microsoft products could be used with them—including browsers other than IE.

Today, we can hypothesize that the Microsoft antitrust decision made it easier for Alphabet, Meta, and Amazon to enter the market. If its products had not forcibly been made interoperable with non-Windows software, Microsoft's internet web search engine Bing, launched in 2009, might have fared better against Google and its MySpace social networking platform could have given Facebook a run for its money. It may even have made Amazon's seemingly unstoppable growth less likely.

But for us as economic observers, Microsoft's "browser wars" saga reflects how regulation can sometimes resuscitate a market. When the US government sought to divide the too-powerful Microsoft, it did so in order to create market competition and act for the well-being of the consumer. To do this it used the 1890 Sherman Antitrust Act, the US government's means of stepping into a market where necessary if one company became too dominant in it. Although the Microsoft case is more than two decades old, we can see some of the same issues occurring again. In September 2022, for example, the EU's long-running antitrust legal procedure against the tech giant Alphabet resulted in a multi-billion dollar fine against Google's parent company for, in a statement issued by the EU's General Court, "[imposing] unlawful restrictions on manufacturers of Android mobile devices and mobile network operators in order to consolidate the dominant position of its search engine."

John Sherman, author of the 1890 Sherman Antitrust Act.

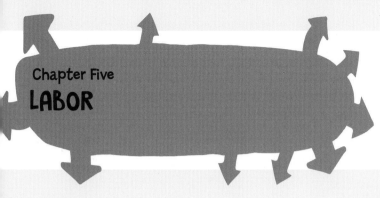

Chapter Five

LABOR

MINIMUM WAGE

COLLECTIVE BARGAINING

UNIONS

LABOR MOBILITY

GENDER PAY GAP

WHAT WE EARN

LABOR MARKETS

ENTREPRENEURS

STRUCTURAL

PARTICIPATION RATES

CREATIVE DESTRUCTION

INCOME INEQUALITY

UNEMPLOYMENT

MEASURING UNEMPLOYMENT

CYCLICAL

FRICTIONAL

SEASONAL

NATURAL RATE

Having focused on businesses, our next step is to take a closer look at the people who work for them. When economists say we are going to labor markets, they really mean who is in the labor force, what we do, and how much we earn. Then, through the entrepreneurs that innovate, they also look at why labor markets change.

THE GENERAL MOTORS CEO

If Mary Barra had been a teenager in 1950, she could have expected to marry and start her own household. Like generations of women before her, she would have continued the tradition of women running a home while her husband left every day to earn a wage. Instead, in 2014, Mary Barra was appointed as CEO of General Motors. She was not just a member of the labor force, she oversaw another 157,000 of its members.

We could have started Barra's story with her childhood interest in cars. However, it really begins with her electrical engineering degree from what was the General Motors Institute (now Kettering University) and continues with an MBA from Stanford University. By 2009, she was running the company's human resources division (a typical female slot). But here, it all changes when she becomes a senior vice president running global product development for General Motors. Ten years later she was GM's CEO.

Car design is her skill set. In the past, she ran engineering divisions and an assembly plant. Now, the decisions that come to her desk relate to a globalized automobile market. She needs to contemplate what will work in the world's high- and middle-income countries. Style or performance, electric or fossil fuels, practicality or excitement are trade-offs she no doubt decides how to balance.

A BASIC CIRCULAR FLOW MODEL

Mary Barra and General Motors take us to labor's past, present, and future. The ideas are relevant far beyond the US. They relate to who is in the labor force, what we earn, and to the entrepreneurs that propel economic growth.

ENTREPRENEUR ▶ *an innovator who propels economic growth by creating new industries.*

WHO IS IN THE LABOR FORCE?
Goods and Services

As one of the three factors of production, labor adds the human input to our land and capital. It attaches the seats to our cars and gives us dental examinations. It is our plumbers, teachers, doctors, and farmers.

But mostly, in the developed world, labor produces services.

Whether looking at the UK, the US, or other higher-income countries, we see that the services slice is the largest piece of the production pie. In the US, for example, the vast majority of workers are engaged in service-producing industries (122 million in 2020, as opposed to 20 million for goods-producing industries—excluding agriculture). Under goods-producing industries, America's Bureau of Labor Statistics (BLS) lists mining, construction, and manufacturing; the list for for service-producing industries is much longer and includes retail, healthcare, and state and local government.

Composition of the labor force

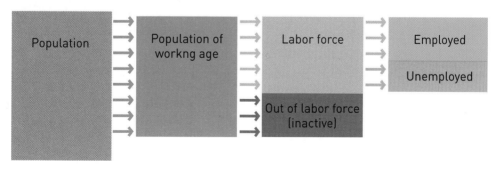

EMPLOYMENT AND UNEMPLOYMENT

A second way to look at the labor force is through its employed and unemployed sectors. By definition, the employed people in the labor force have to be paid. Unemployed, you are in the labor force if you are looking for a job. The age threshold for being counted in the labor force is 16 in the US and the UK; it is 15 in most other places in the world.

We can cite four basic reasons why people are unemployed—cyclical, structural, seasonal, and frictional.

TYPES OF UNEMPLOYMENT

Cyclical
Joblessness rises and falls throughout the business cycle. Predictably, joblessness usually grows when the economy slows or contracts.

Structural
When new industries replace what used to exist, the result is unemployment for the workers with outdated jobs and skills. They experience the impact of the structural change of the economy.

Seasonal
As a year unfolds, certain businesses (leisure and agriculture, for example) need fewer or more employees.

Frictional
When a person leaves a job without yet having found a new one, or a person graduates from school without a place of work to go to, we say that they are experiencing frictional unemployment.

Friction is one reason there is a "natural" rate of unemployment below which joblessness probably will not fall. In recent times, the natural rate of unemployment has hovered between 4 and 5 percent.

PARTICIPATION RATES

A third and final way to see who is working is to look at participation rates. A participation rate records how much of a population produces our goods and services. Defined generally, a participation rate quantifies how much of the population works through the labor force. For the math, we divide the size of the labor force by the entire non-institutionalized civilian population. The US participation rate for those aged 45–54 was 80.7 percent in 2021. For those aged 75 or over it plunged to 8.6 percent. The numbers exclude the child care, elder care, housework, and food and meal preparation done in the home—work that women tend to do.

But more than a number, a participation rate tells a story.

We can use it to better grasp the impact of aging populations. Because life expectancy in developed nations has moved beyond 70 (and past 80 for some countries, including Australia, Japan, and the UK), the labor force will need to support more of the population.

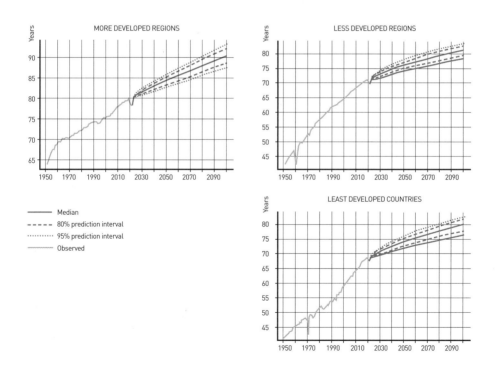

In developed nations, life expectancy has risen to over 75. In less developed nations, life expectancy is around 70. In the least developed world, life expectancy is close to 65.

> **NON-INSTITUTIONALIZED POPULATION ▶** *the whole population excluding people in jail, other correctional facilities, the armed forces, detention centers, and residential care facilities.*

Participation rates also illustrate how women's labor has changed during the past half century. Between 1970 and 2000, women like Mary Barra transformed the workplace. During the years that followed women's initial access to birth control, they increased their labor force participation rates from a 40 percent range to 50 percent (and beyond) in high-income countries. In 2021, US women aged 45–54 had a 75 percent participation rate.

With access to birth control, women could determine when and if they started a family, whether they would leave home for an education or seek employment, get graduate degrees and become doctors, lawyers, and entrepreneurs. The average age at which women married rose, and so did divorce rates.

Acceleration in female labor force participation

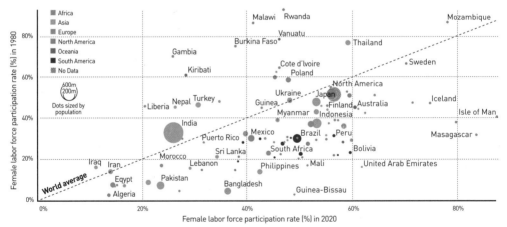

Among the higher-income nations, Iceland and Sweden had the highest female participation rates in 2020.

Still, men's participation rates exceed women's rates. Like the elderly, for the younger members of the labor force, age makes a difference. At the top, with close to a 90 percent rate, in the US, the UK and other high-income countries, are men aged 35–44.

Labor force participation rates by gender—16 Years +

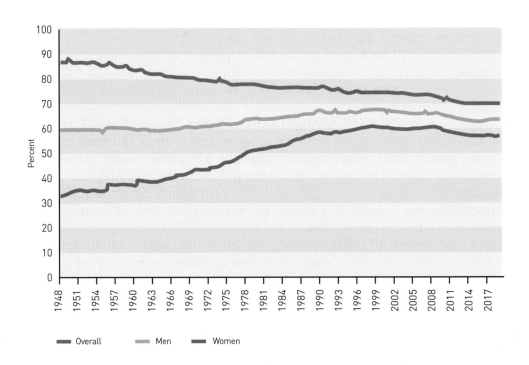

Overall ▬ Men ▬ Women

PARTICIPATION RATE ▶ *the fraction that compares the entire non-institutionalized population (denominator) to the number of workers in the labor force.*

LABOR SUPPLY AND DEMAND

On a labor market graph, the price is your pay and the quantity is the hours people are willing and able to work. Because you are (probably) willing and able to provide more hours of work when the wage or salary is higher, you are on the supply side of a labor market.

> **LABOR MARKETS** ▶ *the process that determines the number of jobs and what workers are paid.*

Supply

Looking more closely at the supply curve, we see many basic economic ideas. Thinking of opportunity cost, you consider what you sacrifice when you accept a wage. Not only might there be some other job that you enjoy but, also, you are sacrificing what others will pay you. In addition, thinking at the margin, you are deciding how many hours you will give to the labor force.

Demand

Meanwhile, the demand side of the market returns us to the margins we thought about in Chapter 1. Aware that margin means something extra, profit-maximizing employers know to keep an eye on marginal cost. They know not to hire extra workers when the expense exceeds the extra revenue they generate. In addition, we have the law of demand. When prices (wages) rise, the quantity demanded for workers goes down.

Putting it all together on a graph, we see a traditional interaction of supply and demand:

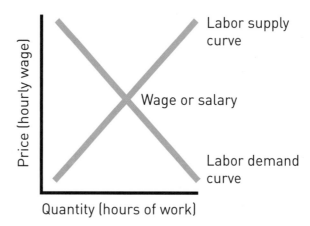

INEQUALITY

While a market determines wages and salaries, we certainly don't all earn the same amount. One economics Nobel laureate commented that the dynamics of capitalism guarantee that our incomes will differ. If we want the incentives that propel economic growth, the trade-off is inequality.

We can assess the income inequality in the US by dividing it into household income quintiles. Then, we see the top 20 percent, with approximately a 53 percent slice of all private household income, earning more than half of the income pie. The US tends toward more income distribution inequality than elsewhere in the developed world.

Then, analytically, we can take the next step with a Gini coefficient. As one of 50 or so metrics we can use to illustrate income inequality, the Gini Index is the most popular. Simply summarized (and skipping some computation), the Gini compares perfectly equal wealth or income distribution to actual distribution. On a graph, it is the area between the line of equality and a curve displaying what quintiles earn or have. Like most metrics, it has flaws that convey inaccurate conclusions. For example, we would not know that a low-income person is a medical student, who is likely to earn far more in the future, or even when the ratios on which a coefficient is based vary, but the math gives us the same final number. Still, we can use it to get the big picture.

The higher the Gini, the more unequal the distribution. Based on 0–1 numbers (or a percent of the equivalent: .22 is 22 percent), a higher number reflects a bigger spread between what the top and bottom earn. Consequently, 0 means everyone is equal while 1 indicates that one party has all the wealth.

In 2022, based on numbers from 2017 to 2020, World Bank statistics displayed the vast Gini differences between Norway (27.7%) and Chile (44.9%).

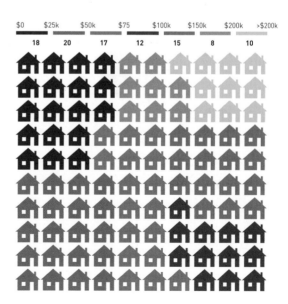

Annual household income	$0	$25k	$50k	$75	$100k	$150k	$200k	>$200k
Percentage of homes	18	20	17	12	15	8	10	

Country	Gini coefficient (%)
Argentina	42.3
Australia	34.3
Canada	33.3
Chile	44.9
France	32.4
India	35.7
Norway	27.7
UK	35.1
US	41.5

Income share of the top 10%, 2021

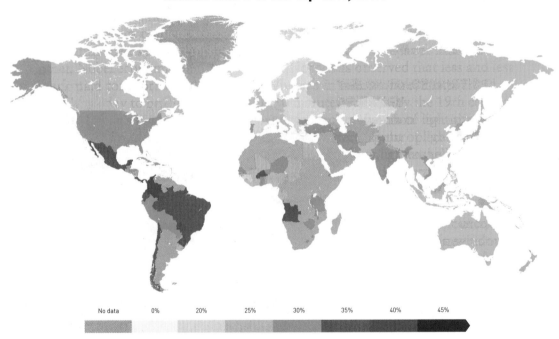

No data	0%	20%	25%	30%	35%	40%	45%

Indeed, where you live can determine the demand for skills in labor markets, a minimum wage mandate, or the power of labor unions. It can shape the distribution of the national income's wages and salaries, rents, interest, and profits. It can also influence how your income will compare to what previous generations earned.

> **GINI COEFFICIENT** ▶ *a number that displays income or wealth inequality.*

Intergenerational Mobility

Looking back and looking forward, as a last step, we can pivot slightly to opportunity. We can ask where and how children are doing better than their parents. The answer is that it depends. As a country, the US is reputedly equal to the UK and less mobile than Australia, Canada, France, Germany, and Sweden. But even between neighborhoods in the same city, the difference can be immense. Recent research from economist Raj Chetty has shown that your neighborhood can make a huge difference.

MINIMUM WAGE

In a 1938 "fireside chat," US President Franklin Roosevelt warned the nation that we cannot "… let any calamity-howling executive with an income of $1,000 a day … tell you … that a wage of $11 a week is going to have a disastrous effect on all American industry." The next day, by signing the Fair Labor Standards Act, he created the first US minimum wage. It began at 25 cents an hour, rose to 30 cents an hour the following year, and by 1945 was 40 cents an hour. In May 1956, it was $1.

Franklin Delano Roosevelt gives one of his "fireside chats" on November 4, 1938.

However, and taking the US as an example, we can show how minimum wage mandates may not always be what they seem. Set at $7.25 in 2009, the US's national minimum wage rate (which some observers pointed out was low

Protests demand a $15 minimum wage in the US.

at the time) has not risen since—and has therefore plunged in value because of inflation. By October 2022, for example, you needed $10.23 to have the same buying power. Fortunately for those on minimum wages, many states and municipalities far exceed the national minimum wage mandate. In some places it is as high as $16 an hour.

Somewhat different from the US, the UK's National Living Wage varies by age and increases every April. In 2022, starting at £4.81 for under-18-year-olds, it climbed to £9.50 an hour for those aged 23 and over. The increases are not solely age-related; economic conditions play a part too, with food prices, the national unemployment rate, and housing costs all factored in. Whereas the US's minimum wage laws date back to the 1930s, the UK's were only introduced in 1998. But in both nations, as well as in other countries that offer minimum wage provisions, any analysis of effectiveness should take into account local purchasing power.

Instead of looking at local and relative purchasing power issues, let us conclude instead with a universal minimum wage debate that looks at the impact of price floors. As we saw in Chapter 3, a price floor is the horizontal line above equilibrium. Some, but not all, economic observers believe that minimum wages (which are a form of a price floor) lead to worker surpluses.

UNEMPLOYMENT RATE ▶ the fraction that compares the number of people in the labor force (denominator) to the people in the labor force that have no job but are looking for one.

One reason for the disagreement is the nature of the research carried out to assess minimum wage effects. In one classic study, Nobel laureate David Card with economist Alan Kreuger compared neighboring communities in two US states when one raised the minimum wage and the other did not. They observed that the higher minimum wage elevated employment rather than eliminated jobs. Because survey results were self-reporting—based on what participants said they did—some question their results.

In Germany, a 2015 minimum wage hike created no significant job losses, although it caused some smaller firms to go out of business. Researchers reported that workers responded to the wage hike by moving to higher-paying jobs in larger firms that were more productive. Those larger firms had a more skilled workforce and more full-time jobs.

David Card, left, and Alan Kreuger, right.

Minimum wages in selected countries

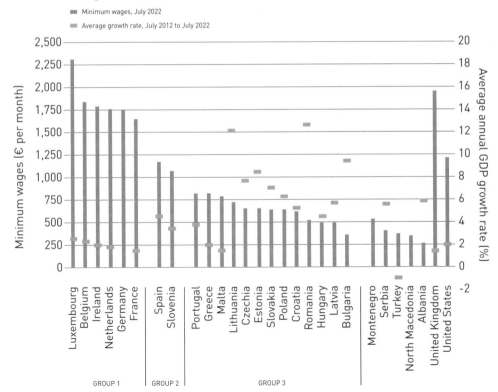

Claudia Goldin.

Gender pay gap in Europe

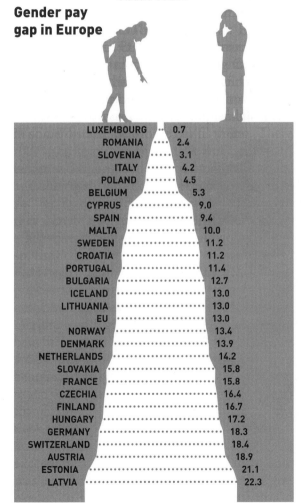

LUXEMBOURG	0.7
ROMANIA	2.4
SLOVENIA	3.1
ITALY	4.2
POLAND	4.5
BELGIUM	5.3
CYPRUS	9.0
SPAIN	9.4
MALTA	10.0
SWEDEN	11.2
CROATIA	11.2
PORTUGAL	11.4
BULGARIA	12.7
ICELAND	13.0
LITHUANIA	13.0
EU	13.0
NORWAY	13.4
DENMARK	13.9
NETHERLANDS	14.2
SLOVAKIA	15.8
FRANCE	15.8
CZECHIA	16.4
FINLAND	16.7
HUNGARY	17.2
GERMANY	18.3
SWITZERLAND	18.4
AUSTRIA	18.9
ESTONIA	21.1
LATVIA	22.3

GENDER PAY GAP

Looking at wages through a gender lens, we would see that women, on average, earn less. According to a UK think tank, the difference is 16 percent less per hour, while the US estimate is 18 percent. But because averages are misleading, we should look at occupations for more of the real story. Using some examples from the US, according to the Institute for Women's Policy Research, in just five out of 120 occupations in the US, women earn more than their male counterparts. At the high side, female producers and directors can enjoy 106.7 percent of what their male counterparts earn, while at the other end, female medical scientists earn only 65.2 percent of the income of their male colleagues.

Even in occupations dominated by women, men earned more in 2020. For elementary school teachers, the median pay for women was 86.2 percent of that of their male counterparts. Similarly, whether a woman was a CEO or a janitor, her earnings were close to 75 percent of what corresponding men made.

Causes

According to Harvard economist Claudia Goldin, a major cause of the gender wage gap is a woman's family-related obligations. Whether it's children, the elderly, or another family member, in American culture the woman has traditionally been the caregiver. Because women have had to be available for caregiving, their pay and promotions have suffered.

Meanwhile, the UK's Institute for Fiscal Studies reminds us that because of the subjects women select during college, they tend to have less future earning power than men after they graduate. By age 25, women are earning five percent less than men. Other sources, though, conclude that women with no children do have equal earning power during their twenties.

So, what women earn and how long they work are determined through labor markets. In those markets, we can say we have people of different ages, religions, and racial cohorts, all with negotiating power.

But there are some people in the labor force who have greater control over what they earn. We could say that they function independently because, as entrepreneurs, they are unique.

ENTREPRENEURS

The word entrepreneur has come a long way. First used by the French during the Middle Ages to describe a military commander, it was applied centuries later to the world of business. Entrepreneurs are, though, more than the people that start their own businesses. They, instead, are the individuals that disrupt. By upsetting the status quo, their innovations eliminate existing industries and create new ones.

However, they cannot do it all alone. They need institutions that act as incentives and support. They benefit from a patent system that gives them a temporary legal monopoly. The antitrust laws that eliminate monopolies also help by encouraging the competitive behaviors that make innovation a necessity. Furthermore, entrepreneurs benefit from viable banking systems that connect savers and borrowers inside and among nations.

We can use the word entrepreneur to describe a group of people. But each of them, because they are entrepreneurs, is unique. So, among the countless individuals who have disrupted our economic world, let's look at two.

Malcom McLean

Our first innovator simply created a box. One that made it possible for US automobile manufacturers such as Mary Barra's General Motors to use cheaply sourced car components, including engine parts, lighting, and assorted electronics, from China.

The box he created was the shipping container.

A typical port during the 1950s looked rather busy and chaotic. The commodities waiting to be loaded onto cargo ships would have come by road or rail. Before and after their journey, people recorded every item on a tally sheet. The longshoreman on the docks could have had more than 100,000 items coming from more than 100 cities in more than 1,000 shipments, ranging from oranges to vehicle parts, destined for one shipload. The entire loading process would have taken six days.

Malcom McLean knew there had to be a better way.

The humble shipping container revolutionized world trade.

As a trucking magnate who bought a fleet of shipping vessels, he perceived the challenge of moving cargo efficiently. Starting with a rusty abandoned tractor trailer, McLean, in 1934, at 21 years old, established the McLean Trucking Company. Within a decade it was a multimillion-dollar concern. An expert cost-cutter, McLean reduced mileages by using the shortest transportation routes possible. He crenellated the exterior of his trucks when he was told that it reduced wind resistance. To boost efficiency, he introduced conveyor belts in a warehouse and switched fuels from gasoline to diesel.

By 1956, as the owner of what became the shipping company Sea-Land, he worked out how to seamlessly connect land and sea. In a shipping first that eventually transformed global trade, on April 26, 1956, beer that had been transported on land in steel boxed containers was not unloaded when it reached the port. Instead, the whole steel container was placed—with the beer still in it—directly onto a ship leaving Newark, New Jersey, and bound for Houston, Texas.

His innovation reduced the cost from $5.83 to approximately 15.8 cents a ton.

It took decades for the ships, ports, truck companies, and railroads to standardize their containers. But it all came together when people were finally able to move the box off a train or a truck onto a new type of boat that was able to carry hundreds of other boxes: a container ship. By 1999, because of the new method that Malcom McLean developed for the transportation of goods, it was possible for the first time to realize a globally-manufactured automobile.

Steve Jobs

During an event after the iPod came out, Steve Jobs said, "This is nothing. Wait till you see what comes next."

He could have been talking about his entire life. Moving from the Apple II to the Macintosh, to Pixar studios, the iPod, iTunes, the iPhone, and the iPad, Steve Jobs gave us the gift of his innovation.

The iPod, one example of innovation from Steve Jobs.

We can see how he impacted product development. For the Apple II case, liking none of the colors he was shown, he considered 2,000 shades of beige. Unsatisfied with the boot-up time for the Macintosh, he inspired the development team to shave 10 seconds off the original prototype. When someone suggested using a wheel for moving through an iPod playlist, he immediately agreed because he saw that it was an elegant alternative to repeatedly pushing a button. He also knew he had to have an iTunes that interconnected with his iMacs and iPods. For the iPhone, he did away with the keyboard completely and demanded that Dupont develop Gorilla Glass for his finger touch interface. The sum of countless examples of innovation, the story of Steve Jobs can be summed up as "what comes next."

Chapter Six
FISCAL POLICY

*Lunch Hours—Fiscal Philosophy—
Spending—Taxes—Borrowing—
Fiscal Expansionary and
Contractionary Policies*

DISCRETIONARY

TRANSFER PAYMENTS

CORPORATION TAX

INCOME TAX

PAYROLL TAXES

LAISSEZ-FAIRE

KEYNESIAN ECONOMICS

SOCIAL SECURITY

MANDATORY

TAXATION

DEFICIT

SPENDING

BORROWING

FISCAL POLICY

DEBT

HEALTHCARE

REDISTRIBUTION

PHILLIPS CURVE

AGGREGATE DEMAND AND SUPPLY

In the circular flow model, our next stop is government. Whether looking at a president or a prime minister, Congress or Parliament, we see a government that spends, taxes, and borrows. Called fiscal policy, spending, taxation, and borrowing fund programs and steer the economy.

LUNCH HOURS

One US citizen who worked in France expressed her surprise with the country's lunchtime rules. Not only was she prohibited from working during lunch, but her colleagues happily complied. Reflecting more of a US ethos, she tried to sneak in some work as she ate.

Her professional team demonstrated a work/leisure attitude that articulates a broader French fiscal fabric. Their government implements a high level of social spending that supports the quality of life as fiscal policy. The French approach creates a slew of trade-offs that we will consider as we define fiscal policy and see the economic metrics that have very real social implications.

FISCAL PHILOSOPHY

We could say that fiscal policy starts with your philosophy. If you support a less active role for government, less spending, and less taxing, then your philosophy is more similar to the classical economists that champion the laissez-faire of Adam Smith. But if you believe that free markets need a nudge from government to create a more equal society and fuel economic growth, your alternative is the social programs and higher tax rates that facilitate spending and redistribution from the more affluent to those with less. Philosophically, you have moved closer to what the 1930s economist John Maynard Keynes described. While we will look more closely at Keynesian economics at the end of this chapter, for now we just need to know that it represents more government.

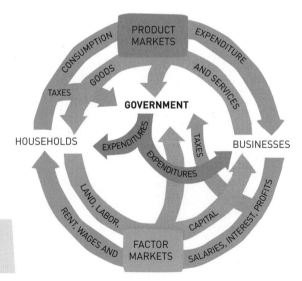

FISCAL POLICY ▶ *government's* *spending, taxing, and borrowing.*

Looking closely at fiscal policy takes us to three basics. We can see how governments spend and tax. And from there, we can consider what they need to borrow.

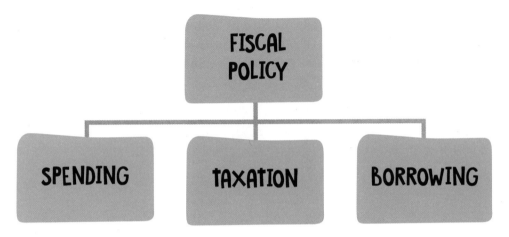

SPENDING

If a country's budget is a spending pie, the slices comprising it can be classed as mandatory and discretionary. Perpetuated through long-lasting legislation because they continue year after year, the mandatory sections are required. By contrast, discretionary spending can be more fleeting. It can go up or down, or be eliminated from a nation's annual finances.

DISCRETIONARY EXPENDITURES ▶ *the optional budget spending that is not required by law.*

MANDATORY EXPENDITURES ▶ *fiscal policy spending that is required by law.*

Mandatory Spending

In the US, the mandatory budget items are primarily entitlements and interest payments. As transfer payments, entitlements are not provided in return for any good or service. We receive them because of circumstances that include health, age, and job status.

In 1935, steering the US through the Great Depression, President Franklin Roosevelt proposed a measure to provide the income security that people needed at that moment. The main provision of the act was the retiree payments that could start at age 65 for most recipients. It also sent support to fatherless families and the unemployed. To ensure widespread approval, Roosevelt included no income criteria. The social security system has been a feature of government spending in the US ever since.

Franklin D. Roosevelt signs the Social Security Act in 1935.

TRANSFER PAYMENT ▶ *money disbursed by government to individuals because of circumstance, rather than as a payment for a good or a service.*

The US budget is split between mandatory and discretionary spending, with the former dominated by entitlement spending. Occupying close to three quarters of the spending pie, this is composed of Social Security that mostly goes to retirees but also includes people with disabilities. The Medicare entitlement that can cover doctors, hospital stays, and pharmaceuticals targets people aged 65 and older. Meanwhile, allocated to lower-income individuals, the medical care paid for by Medicaid is shared between the federal government and individual states.

ENTITLEMENTS ▶ *budget items that many people expect government will provide, such as healthcare.*

Still, as a percentage of GDP, the US is among the relatively small spenders on individuals. Like Switzerland, the US allocates proportionally less of its GDP on individual spending than Denmark and Sweden.

Social spending (highest and lowest)

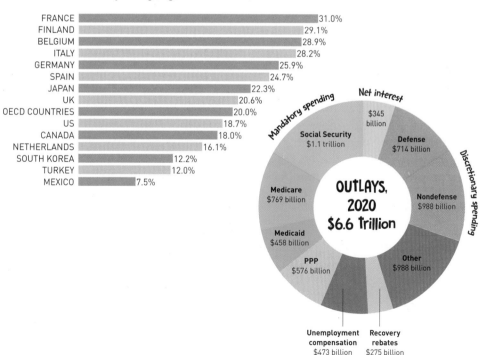

FRANCE	31.0%
FINLAND	29.1%
BELGIUM	28.9%
ITALY	28.2%
GERMANY	25.9%
SPAIN	24.7%
JAPAN	22.3%
UK	20.6%
OECD COUNTRIES	20.0%
US	18.7%
CANADA	18.0%
NETHERLANDS	16.1%
SOUTH KOREA	12.2%
TURKEY	12.0%
MEXICO	7.5%

Mandatory spending · Net interest

OUTLAYS, 2020 $6.6 Trillion

Net interest $345 billion

Defense $714 billion

Discretionary spending

Social Security $1.1 trillion

Nondefense $988 billion

Medicare $769 billion

Medicaid $458 billion

Other $988 billion

PPP $576 billion

Unemployment compensation $473 billion

Recovery rebates $275 billion

Safety nets

However, when we use words like mandatory and discretionary, or even the terms social spending and safety net, we are summarizing the disparate approaches of many countries and billions of people. Being more precise, by comparing US medical spending to the UK and France, we can get a better idea of how nations differ.

The US has what we might call a mixed system. Through employment, the US labor force can get private insurance. But also, with an Affordable Care Act passed in 2010, private insurance exchanges were established. Then, with Medicare, the US has a government-run, single payer private provider system for (most of the) people aged 65 and older. And still adding to the mix, they have varied state Medicaid programs targeting low-income individuals and a government system of hospitals for veterans.

Great Britain has the purest approach to socialized medicine. With government financing care, and providing it, its slice of the budget is massive. In 2017, approximately 80 percent of all healthcare spending in the UK came from the government. As a mandatory budget item, it is a dominant slice of the budget pie.

Finally, to add yet another approach, we can return to France where everyone buys health insurance and can expect public insurance to cover as much as 80 percent of costs. As a result, out-of-pocket payments are relatively minimal. In perhaps the antithesis of the US system, the French government, ranging from the number of hospital beds to the number of medical students, makes many of the healthcare decisions for public hospitals and care.

You can see that in many ways we are comparing apples and oranges. Yes, we can get a general impression of who does more and who does less social spending. But the names of programs and their textures vary considerably. We can say, though, that the US's fiscal obligations for social insurance are less developed and less broad than most of the EU's 27 countries.

Net interest

For all nations that have borrowed money by selling bonds to individuals, businesses, banks, and governments, we can expect interest payments to be a budget item. When interest rates rise, as during 2022, so too will the budgetary expense.

COVID debt

COVID spending added trillions to most national budgets. For the US, the 2020 Paycheck Protection Program (PPP) enabled businesses to apply for the assistance that would let them continue paying employees. But the US was not alone. Combined with other COVID programs, the cost of this support boosted global borrowing. Now, countries not only have to repay the loans but they also have mandatory interest obligations until the debts mature.

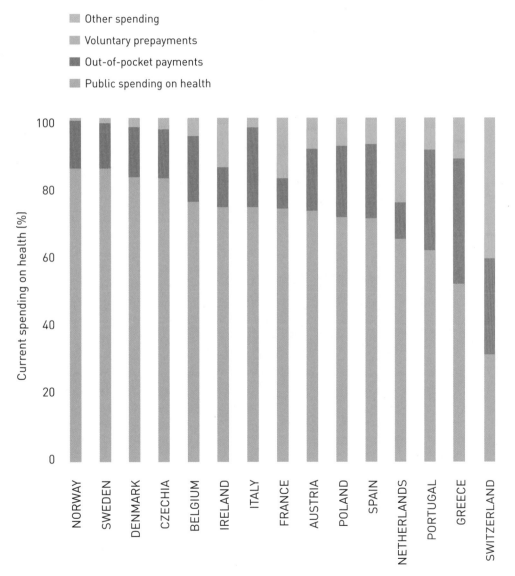

- Other spending
- Voluntary prepayments
- Out-of-pocket payments
- Public spending on health

The length of the green bars displays a small or large role for government.

Discretionary spending

Topped by defense, each item in the long list of discretionary spending categories is hypothetically optional. The list ranges from government administration and international affairs to education and homeland security. It includes tax collection and securities regulation.

As one of the largest budget spending categories, defense spending is a massive slice in the discretionary part of the budget pie.

TAXES

Comparing tax systems, an exact comparison is impossible among high-income nations. But we can say that your spending philosophy directly impacts tax policy. If you favored the classical side, then less government should mean lower taxes. Supporting fewer government programs, you have less to pay for. Consequently, in 2020, you probably would have been hesitant about implementing a Paycheck Protection Program. By contrast, as a Keynesian who perceived the pandemic as a threat to a healthy GDP, your cure would have been the PPP.

Whatever your philosophy, though, you still need to decide who pays more and who pays less. With progressive tax systems the wealthy bear a greater burden, while a regressive approach takes more from those that have less. Then, sort of in the middle, we have proportional taxation with the same percentage for everyone.

Progressive Taxation

With a progressive approach, the more affluent pay a higher percent. One example in the

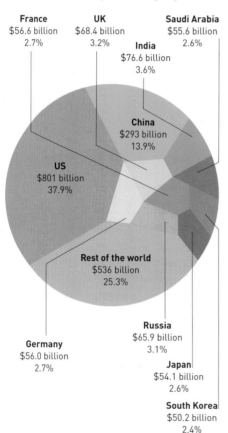

The World's Top Military Spenders

France
$56.6 billion
2.7%

UK
$68.4 billion
3.2%

Saudi Arabia
$55.6 billion
2.6%

India
$76.6 billion
3.6%

China
$293 billion
13.9%

US
$801 billion
37.9%

Rest of the world
$536 billion
25.3%

Russia
$65.9 billion
3.1%

Germany
$56.0 billion
2.7%

Japan
$54.1 billion
2.6%

South Korea
$50.2 billion
2.4%

United States is the individual income tax. The marginal tax rate for someone earning $50,000 a year is lower than the rate for a $100,000 earner.

By marginal tax rates, we are referring to brackets of income that have different tax rates. In 2022, for someone who earned $539,900 and filed individually, any income at that amount or higher was taxed at a 37 percent rate. For that same person, income between $215,950 and $539,900 had a 35 percent rate. As the income declined, so too did the rate until it shrunk to 10 percent at $0 to $10,000.

Like the US, most other high-income countries have a progressive individual income tax approach.

Regressive

A second possibility is having the people who earn less pay a higher percentage of their income. But that does not happen, at least for income tax. It does, however, take place at the supermarket and the gas station. If gas is taxed at a dollar a gallon, then filling up a tank might mean a $12 tax tab for everyone, rich or poor. Consequently, if you earn $50 a year, that $12 is 24 percent of your income. But if you take home $100, then it's 12 percent.

Proportional

Finally, a third possibility is proportional taxation. Proportional taxes take the same percentage from everyone. In the United States, everyone pays a Medicare tax that takes 2.9 percent (or 1.45 percent when your employer pays half) from your income.

As you can see, in 2020, the US government received the most revenue from individual income taxes. However, the payroll taxes that mostly fund Social Security and Medicare also take a hefty chunk.

US State and Local Taxes

Because the US also has state and local taxes, how you are taxed depends on where you live. While most states depend on an income tax for their revenue, six states do not. Instead, they raise revenue through sales taxes.

Global Spending and Taxes

Taking the leap from US to the world, we can return to the Organization for Economic Cooperation and Development (OECD). While in the United States individual income tax is a major source of government revenue, other governments look elsewhere. Most OECD countries depend more on consumption taxes such as VAT.

VAT

Not levied in the Unites States, VAT (Value Added Tax) is an important revenue stream for most other developed countries. VAT is what its name indicates: it taxes the value added to each stage of a good's production. So, if a pretzel started as wheat, then became flour, and after that a pretzel, its producers and then the consumer would have paid the tax. Vastly oversimplifying, we could imagine 10 percent VAT at each stage. We can also call VAT regressive, because everyone purchasing the same item pays the same amount.

Incentives

About more than the money we pay, taxes create incentives. They can help us decide where to live. Some people suggest the exodus of people from New Jersey to Florida is because New Jersey has a high income tax while Florida has none. The French financial newspaper Les Echos reported that more people whose annual income exceeded 100,000 euros left France between 2012 and 2013 than those on lower incomes. Whereas the overall French migration rate was close to 6 percent, the high-earner departure rate was at least 40 percent.

Also affecting our behavior, a high tax on soda or cigarettes can make us buy less. In addition, tax breaks encourage us to buy a house when we get a mortgage tax deduction. It is even possible that a high income tax encourages us to work less.

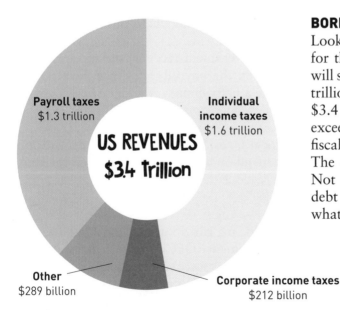

US REVENUES $3.4 Trillion

Payroll taxes
$1.3 trillion

Individual income taxes
$1.6 trillion

Other
$289 billion

Corporate income taxes
$212 billion

BORROWING

Looking back at the numbers for the US 2020 budget, you will see that outlays total $6.6 trillion and revenue is close to $3.4 trillion. When spending exceeds revenue during one fiscal year, we have a deficit. The debt is a little different. Not an annual number, the debt is a cumulative record of what a country owes.

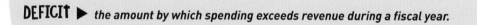

DEBT ▶ *the total amount that the federal government owes.*

Deficits

There are actually two kinds of deficits: cyclical and structural. Relating to the ups and downs of the economy, cyclical deficits are shortlived. Because of a decrease in GDP, job losses accelerate the decline in tax revenue. The government has to spend more for the unemployed while collecting less revenue. The result is a deficit caused by the business cycle.

Much more stubborn, structural deficits are the result of ongoing spending. Whether the economy is strong or weak, the UK will spend on the National Health Service and the US will continue to make Social Security and Medicare provisions. As a fundamental part of UK government spending, the cost of the NHS is structural.

It is entirely possible to have a cyclical and a structural deficit. But the structual deficit is the big worry.

DEFICIT ▶ *the amount by which spending exceeds revenue during a fiscal year.*

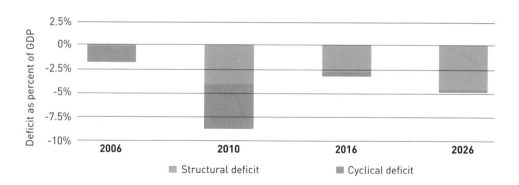

Shown by the gray bar, the US cyclical deficit followed the December 2007–June 2009 recession.

The Debt

When we borrow because of a deficit, typically the national debt will grow. But the big question is whether the debt has become too large. Three criteria give us an answer:

1. Robust growth: we can determine if economic growth is sufficient and sustained.
2. Independent economic institutions: we should be sure that economic institutions like the central bank and monetary policy are independent.
3. Low interest rates: we should note if the level of interest rates on the debt is sufficiently low.

But the big number that captures the size of a country's borrowing is its debt-to-GDP ratio. Somewhat like deciding if a mortgage is too big, we can judge whether a national debt is excessive by comparing it to a barometer of national wealth—GDP. If a person who earns $200,000 annually borrows $5 million to buy a house, they have probably overextended themselves. But if Bill Gates borrowed the same amount, as a billionaire he could manage the loan and pay it back quite easily. Similarly, affluent countries can borrow more. However, when the amount exceeds 100 percent of the GDP, it may have borrowed too much.

Debt-to-GDP Ratios, 2021

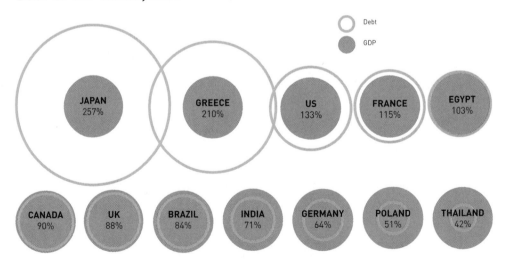

US borrowing started during the American Revolution. Needing the money to fight the war, the Continental Congress and individual states borrowed money by selling bonds. When the war ended, the big problem was how to pay back what had been borrowed. The Secretary of the Treasury, Alexander Hamilton, knew that to borrow in the future he needed to fund the debt. Through his development plan, he worked out how. For centuries, nations have been borrowing to fund wars in an entirely similar way.

FISCAL EXPANSIONARY AND CONTRACTIONARY POLICIES

Beyond decisions about where to spend a federal budget, fiscal policy tells us whether to spend. When, for example, unemployment rates increase, fiscal policy can provide a solution. A government can initiate projects that create jobs. Or, like the US during the COVID pandemic, it can establish a Paycheck Protection Plan that puts money in people's pockets. Correspondingly, government buoys individual wealth when it lowers taxes. But then, if inflation is an economic malady with prices rising too much and too quickly, the fiscal cure is less government spending and higher taxes.

As economists, we can illustrate fiscal policy on a graph of aggregate demand and aggregate supply. Our axes are the price level and real output. A line representing aggregate or total demand in an economy is created by consumer, business, and government spending, and net exports (exports minus imports). Its aggregate supply relates to what businesses spend on land, labor, and capital. The equilibrium intersection where both lines meet expresses national output and the price level.

Here we can find the level that is just right. If national production of goods and services and prices is at the right level, fiscal policy can remain constant. However, if inflation is too high, then policy makers need to shift the aggregate demand curve to the left. Increasing taxes or diminishing spending would be

AGGREGATE DEMAND ▶ shifted by changes in spending on final products, aggregate demand shows how much buyers—consumers, businesses, government, and net exports—purchase at different prices and output levels.

AGGREGATE SUPPLY ▶ shifted by changes in land, labor, and capital, aggregate supply shows how much suppliers produce at different prices and output levels.

the policy prescription. In contrast, if employment and economic growth were too low then aggregate demand needs to shift to the right. (Although fiscal policy can manipulate the aggregate supply curve, we need to wait for our next chapter to see how monetary policy and interest rates relate.) In this situation, more spending and lower taxes are the answers.

Returning to Chapter 1, we can see the same phenomena on a production possibilities (PP) graph. Then, fiscal policy can move a dot signaling underutilization. Lowering taxes gives consumers and businesses more to spend on goods and services. Correspondingly, when government repairs roads and upgrades a transportation infrastructure, it boosts economic activity. On the AD/AS graph, the AD line shifts to the right. The result? Output and the price level go up. On a PP graph, the dot moves closer to the PP line.

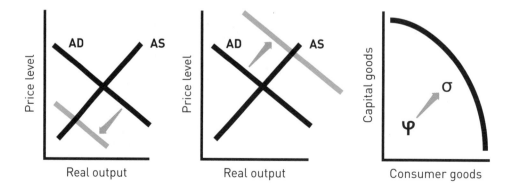

The need to pay for the war against Britain led to borrowing by the Continental Congress and the establishment of the US National Debt.

Chapter Seven
MONETARY POLICY

Inventing Money—The Characteristics of Money—The Money Supply—Central Banks—A Central Bank Toolkit—The Anthropology of Money

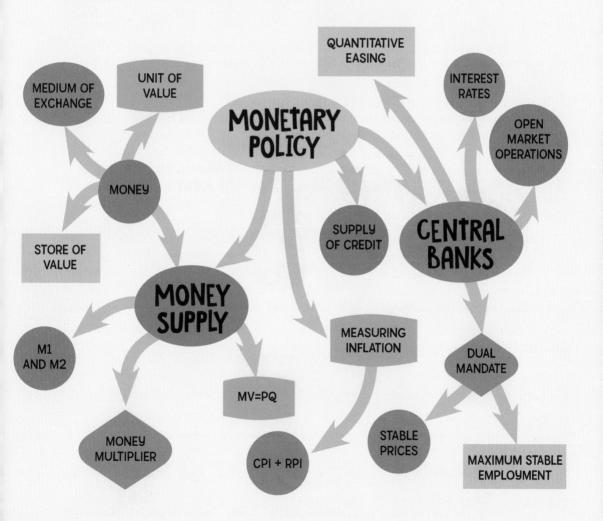

Returning to the circular flow model, we will remain with government for a second stop. This time our destination is money and credit. Through their monetary policy, governments influence economic activity by deciding whether there should be more or less money and credit moving around the circular flow.

INVENTING MONEY

A thousand or so years ago, when doing business in China you might have used copper disks with a square hole cut out of their center to pay for goods and services. The hole allowed the disks to be threaded on long pieces of string, so that they looked rather like necklaces. What you were able to buy depended on how many strings you carried.

At some point, China's merchants decided there had to be a better way of doing business. They began leaving their strings of copper disks in what were known as "deposit shops," receiving in return a paper receipt displaying the value of the disks the shop was holding for them.

Soon the government took over the deposit shops and became responsible for issuing the paper receipts—which we would today call paper money.

Coins from Song Dynasty China, c. 1100 BCE, with punched "string holes."

THE CHARACTERISTICS OF MONEY

To function as money, a rectangular piece of paper, a cow, a seashell, or some other commodity needs to have three characteristics: it should serve as a medium of exchange, a unit of value, and a store of value.

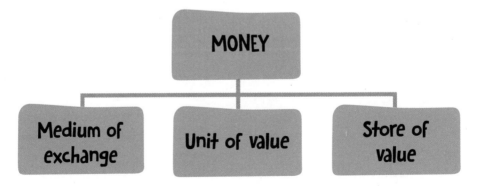

Medium of Exchange

Imagine offering to pay a dentist with your sweater. The dentist would say no. She might like the sweater, but she would not be able to use it to buy toothpaste or pay her staff because sweaters are not a medium of exchange. Unacceptable for two sides of countless transactions, the sweater is not a "mediator."

As a medium of exchange, money removes the need for barter. It expands the potential of dowries and other family transactions. It does eliminate the need for a "double coincidence of wants." Instead, we wind up with a market in which the medium of exchange enables both us and many others to sell what we own and buy what we want. We don't have to find each other.

The owners of the pigs, the grapes, and the eggs do not need to locate each other. They just need the market.

Owns grapes, wants pig

Owns eggs, wants pig

MARKET

Owns pig, wants grapes

Owns grapes, wants eggs

Unit of Value

In addition, as money, commodities have a value that most people are aware of. We know what represents a high price and what is low. Then, recognizing that a 5-euro t-shirt could be poorly made and a 200-euro concert ticket is expensive, we can make a decision. As buyers, we can determine whether a good or a service is worth the sacrificed alternative purchases we could make for the same amounts. Correspondingly, as producers, we can decide what we are willing and able to spend on land, labor, and capital. Having the common unit of currency lets us compare. It lets money send a message.

Store of Value

The third requisite for an item to be money relates to the future. Money needs to retain value. If we don't spend it today, we want it to have similar purchasing power tomorrow or next year. Being able to store value enables saving and

Even when these limestone disks were too heavy to be transported, and even when one of them was dropped into the Pacific Ocean, their owners on the Micronesian island of Yap continued to use them as money.

dependable pricing. In nations like Venezuela with sky-high rates of inflation, because money won't store value, people do not save it.

As you might expect, the three attributes of money relate to each other. When money won't store value, we use it as little as possible. Consequently, it is no longer a medium of exchange nor a unit of value.

THE MONEY SUPPLY

Next, we need to ask, "How much?"

Having accepted a commodity as money, governments like to know how much of it is circulating. Because money need not be tangible, money supply totals include more than the cash we can place in a wallet. Called M1, the US money supply, for example, includes currency, demand deposits, and other liquid deposits.

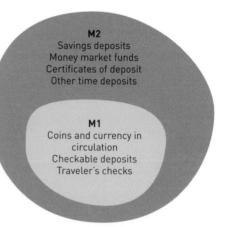

M2
Savings deposits
Money market funds
Certificates of deposit
Other time deposits

M1
Coins and currency in
circulation
Checkable deposits
Traveler's checks

LIQUIDITY ▶ *the extent to which an investment can become money.*

The key word here is *liquid*. M1 includes the most liquid forms of money—the kinds that are most easily spendable. For that reason, currency and coins are in M1, as are demand deposit checking accounts.

However, M1 is only the beginning. Sometimes, we can call M2 the money supply. Not only does M2 include M1, but also less liquid forms of money like the fixed-term deposits (also known as time deposits) that we retain in order to earn interest. Then, in the third-most-liquid category, we have other checkable deposits like our money market deposit accounts. All are mediums of exchange, and units and stores of value.

At this point, you might be wondering if your credit or debit card is money. The answer is No. Based on an M1 and M2 definition of money, neither your credit card nor your debit card is money. Instead, money is the commodity they access for payment.

CENTRAL BANKS

Returning to our circular flow model, we can think about the movement of money around the outer loop. As payment for goods and services, the supply of money and credit affects how much an economy produces. To be sure that the appropriate amounts of money and credit move around the circular flow, countries create central banks. While central banks have an assortment of responsibilities that relate to financial transactions, their most important job is monetary policy decisions about money and credit.

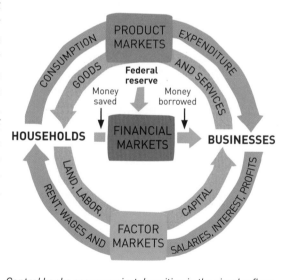

Central banks occupy a pivotal position in the circular flow.

MONETARY POLICY ▶ *overseen by central banks, monetary policy targets the supply of money and credit in an economy.*

The US Federal Reserve.

The Federal Reserve

The United States decided it needed a central bank after a 1907 banking crisis. Then, because of bank failures, bank runs, and unsettled markets, the financial sector looked to the world's leading banker to solve its problems. Rising to the occasion, J.P. Morgan held a series of meetings in his library during which he dictated what everyone had to do. When the crisis began to subside, concerns were voiced as to why a private citizen was overseeing monetary policy.

The result was a new federal agency. The equivalent of a central bank, the Federal Reserve was created in 1913. It had a Chair, 12 regional banks, and, subsequently, a body called the Federal Open Market Committee (the FOMC) that had more direct control over implementing policy. Most crucially, the Fed, as it came to be known, was supposed to be independent, unencumbered by politics.

More recently, it has been given a dual mandate. The Federal Reserve is supposed to maintain stable prices and maximize employment. The problem is that achieving more of one has the opportunity cost of benefiting the other. We will soon see why.

DUAL MANDATE ▶ *the main goals of the US Federal Reserve are stable prices and maximum employment.*

The European Central Bank (ECB)

Similar to the Federal Reserve, the ECB's mandate is to maintain price stability. Very different from the Fed, though, the ECB's authority extends beyond national borders. Its existence began with and depends on Europe's monetary union. One goal of the monetary union was to boost economic activity by reducing friction. Like physics, monetary friction slows financial transactions. The euro and a single monetary policy eliminated the friction of converting and coordinating different currencies.

That takes us to June 1, 1998, when the ECB was created, and to 1999, for the introduction of the euro. At the top of a monetary hierarchy, the ECB directly manages the euro and "frames and implements EU economic and monetary policy." The ECB has an Executive Board and a General Council. Composed of six ECB Executive Board members and 19 governors of the euro-area national banks, its Governing Council sets monetary policy for the euro area. Whereas the General Council is advisory, the Executive Board makes day-to-day decisions. When decisions come from the ECB Council, national banks in eurozone countries implement them.

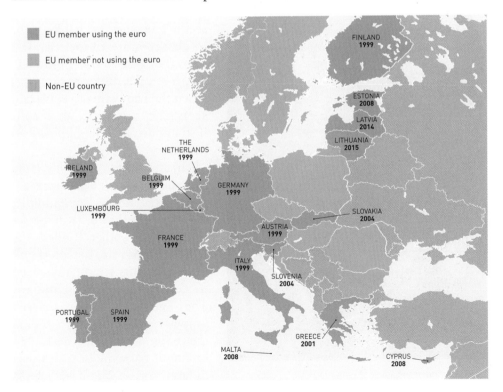

Bank of England

While the US got its central bank because of a crisis and the ECB was a by-product of monetary union, the UK's central bank was created when, more than 300 years ago, England needed money to fight a war against France. Founded in 1694, the Bank of England (which was originally a private enterprise) has been servicing the British government ever since and guiding the UK's monetary policy.

In 1997, the Bank of England was given political independence.

A CENTRAL BANK TOOLKIT

All central banks have a toolkit they use in order to perform their operations. Let's look at the one used by the Federal Reserve.

First, we might see the discount rate. As the interest rate that the Federal Reserve charges banks, the discount rate gives the Fed the power to affect the interest rates that the banks charge you and me. After all, as profit-seeking businesses, banks want to charge more to their lenders than they pay to obtain money. As a tool, the discount rate rises when the Fed wants to constrain economic activity and it falls if they decide the opposite is necessary.

In addition to controlling the discount rate, the Fed "targets" other rates. It tries, for example, to affect the rate that banks charge each other. Called the federal funds rate, the interbank rate represents what banks need to exceed when lending money. The Fed also might borrow money overnight by selling the bank a security and then buying it back the next day at a different price. The basic idea is

The Founding of the Bank of England.

to establish a minimum rate. Then, if banks want to be profitable, they have to charge more than they paid the Fed. With both approaches—reserve interest and overnight loans—the Fed is establishing the rate that banks charge each other. Then, from that key rate, all other rates ripple outwards.

FINANCIAL INTERMEDIARIES ▶ *the institutions that enable savers and borrowers to interact.*

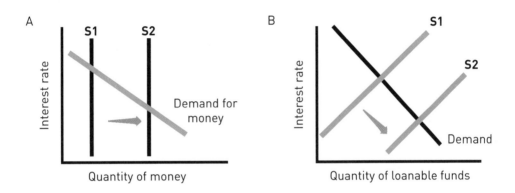

Responding to a recession, in graph A, the Fed decided it wanted to decrease interest rates and increase the money supply. So, it reached into its toolkit to be sure that banks had the incentive to make more money available. As in graph B, a shifting supply curve (S1 and S2) of loanable funds brought banks' interest rates down.

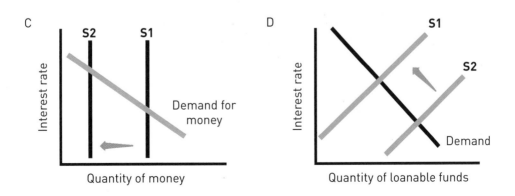

Responding to excessive inflation, in graph C, the Fed decided it wanted to increase interest rates and decrease the money supply. So, it reached into its toolkit to be sure that the supply of loanable funds decreased. As in graph D, a shifting supply curve of loanable funds brought banks' interest rates up.

Beyond its three basic tools, the Fed, through its open market operations, can inject more money into or direct money out of banks. All we need to think of here are bank deposits. When the Fed sells a security, someone has to withdraw money from a bank account to buy it. As a result, that bank has fewer loanable funds. By contrast, when the Fed buys bonds from individuals and businesses, it sends more money into banks, thereby increasing what they can loan to people. (Here, just think "Buy, Boost" and "Sell, Sink.")

Lastly, the Fed's newest tool came in handy during the December 2007–June 2009 recession, when it needed to jumpstart lending. Having just undergone a housing crisis, the banks preferred to buy government securities with their reserves rather than loan them to businesses and individuals. The Fed knew that the banking system needed a nudge. So, it purchased worthless securities the banks had on their balance sheets to inject more money into the system. Then it bought government bonds to increase their prices and thereby lower their interest rates. Once the banks could no longer earn enough from government securities, they had to make loans to generate some profits. The process was called quantitative easing (QE). Subsequently, in 2022, when the Fed needed to rein in activity and sell its securities, there was quantitative tightening (QT).

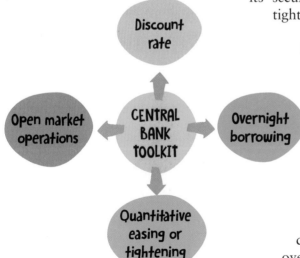

Money Creation

Here, though, is where it becomes really interesting.

Like a magician, banks can create money out of thin air. They just need to make a loan that adds to M1. Assume for example that the Fed buys a $100 bond. As a result, Bank A receives a $100 deposit from the seller. Vastly oversimplifying, we could say at this point that the money supply has

> **MONEY MULTIPLIER ▶** *the number that shows how many times the reserves created by a deposit increase the money supply when they move through the banking system as a succession of deposits and loans.*

$100 and the bank has more money in its reserves. Then, because of that extra money, they decide to loan someone else $90. That $90 is withdrawn from the bank and deposited in Bank B.

So, we now have $100 in Bank A and $90 in Bank B. Magically, the money supply became $190. As this process unfolds, from bank to bank, we get what is called the money multiplier. Just as its name indicates, the money multiplier is the process through which the supply of money grows because of a sequence of deposits and loans.

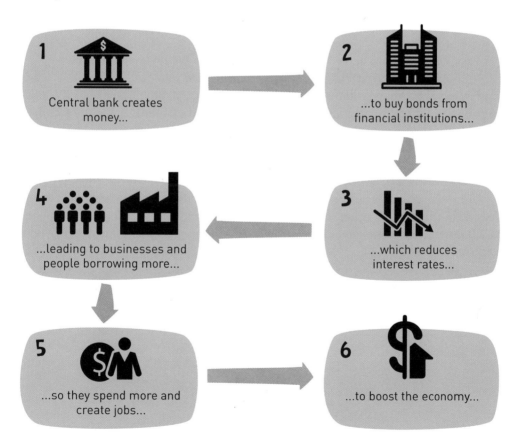

1. Central bank creates money...

2. ...to buy bonds from financial institutions...

3. ...which reduces interest rates...

4. ...leading to businesses and people borrowing more...

5. ...so they spend more and create jobs...

6. ...to boost the economy...

Inflation

The mandate of all three central banks we have looked at includes price stability. All recognize the dangers of inflation. Like fiscal policy but with a different toolkit, the central banks try to rein in inflation. Their basic approach targets the business and consumer purchasing activity that responds to interest rates.

Perhaps even more serious than unemployment, out-of-control inflation upsets all economic activity. Returning to the three basic characteristics of money, inflation constrains the ability of currency to serve as a unit of value, a medium of exchange, and a store of value.

As for its cause, not all economists agree. Some say we have three causes of inflation:

1. Cost push: when the cost of businesses' land, labor, and/or capital go up, then prices tend to rise.
2. Demand pull: when too many dollars or euros or pounds from consumers chase too few goods and services, then prices tend to rise.
3. Unitary sources: when one group elevates the price of a widely used commodity like oil, prices tend to rise.

Others say that inflation is solely a monetary phenomenon. We can summarize what this group—the monetarists—believe with a formula called the equation of exchange. According to the equation of exchange, $MV=PQ$. MV is the money side of the equation with M equaling the money supply and V standing for velocity. By velocity, we just mean the number of times the same unit of money (like the dollar or the euro) is spent. After all, when I buy a t-shirt, the retailer could use my dollars or euros to pay employees who then spend that money at other establishments that pay their workers, who spend it. Meanwhile, P is the general price level and Q refers to the quantity of goods and services produced.

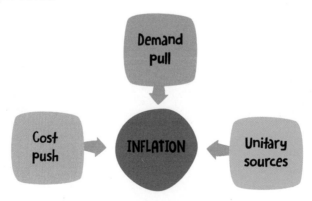

Because monetarists believe V is relatively constant, we have M becoming a crucial determinant of the price level and quantity of goods and services represented by PQ. Knowing that MV is what we spend and PQ is what we produce, too much M can push the prices up in PQ. Too little can constrain production. Just right, and we have ideal economic growth. Citing the lag between a government's monetary policy and its impact, monetarists oppose discretionary monetary policy. Instead, they suggest an automatic money supply increase that annually approximates 3–6 percent.

EQUATION OF EXCHANGE ▶ stated as MV=PQ, an equation that displays the influence of the money supply on output when the velocity of money is relatively stable.

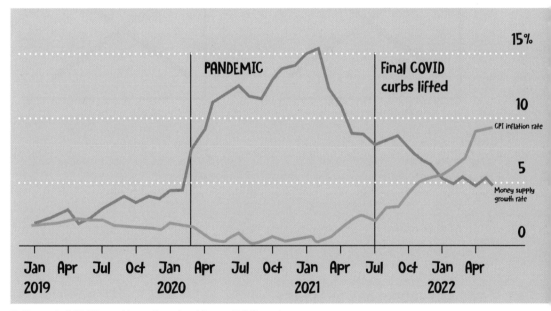

Believers in MV=PQ would say that after M rose, P followed.

On the other hand, we have the Keynesians who say the monetary policy target should be interest rates. Recalling John Maynard Keynes from Chapter 6, we can think of the business investment activity he sought to encourage or restrain. For Keynes, interest rates, which are the cost of borrowing, were at the center of a central bank's targets. As a result, central banks need to elevate interest rates during excessive inflation and lower them to end a recession.

During 2022, central banks used interest rate rises to fight their inflation maladies. After rates touched historic lows, central bankers raised them to fight inflation.

On our AD/AS graphs, we can illustrate the central bankers' goals. When higher interest rates lead to less business activity, as AD moves to the left, the price level sinks and inflation moderates. But we sacrifice more output. On the other hand, if a central bank lowers interest rates, the AD line shifts to the right. Then we wind up with more output but also an elevated price level.

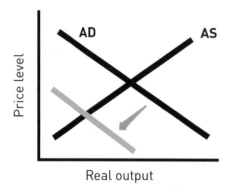
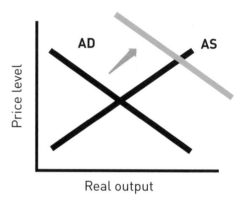

When monetary policy fights inflation, AD (aggregate demand) shifts to the left, and lowers real output and the price level.

When monetary policy fights recession, AD shifts to the right, and elevates output and the price level.

At this point, we can step back a bit. Yes, money affects economic activity. But it also does so much more. We need only look at the anthropology of money.

THE ANTHROPOLOGY OF MONEY
Money reflects power.

When governments establish central banks, they are demonstrating their authority. The money the central banks print and control the supply of becomes an expression of national power. Think of how the US dollar is now a form of universal currency, used and valued around the world and not just in America—and how this contributes to the prestige of the United States internationally. Or why, when it was a colonial power, Britain placed images of its monarchs on the currency of the overseas territories it controlled—and why, after independence, most of those territories replaced on their currency the images of their faraway ex-monarchs with local political leaders and cultural icons.

Money conveys values.

Some time around 2030, the US plans to remove from the $20 bill the image of the dead, white president Andew Jackson, and replace it with the face of Harriet Tubman, who, as a black woman, former enslaved person, Union spy, and suffragette, was pretty much the exact opposite of the US's seventh chief executive. Amongst other things, this is a very public statement of the country's changing attitudes toward women, people of color, and social activists.

From 2017, Norway began to redesign its banknotes so that they displayed images that emphasized the country's strong links to the sea and which show lighthouses, ships, fish, and crashing waves—with no faces of kings, queens, politicians, composers, or authors anywhere in sight. This is because Norway recognizes that its fortunes and its identity are intimately tied to its relationship with the sea, and it wants to display that on its currency.

A prototype of the $20 bill featuring Harriet Tubman.

As the denominations on Norway's banknotes increase, so too does the intensity of the sea-based imagery it displays: from a reassuring, welcoming lighthouse on the lowest-value 50-kroner note to an untamed, roaring ocean on the highest-value 1,000-kroner note.

A pre-independence Indian Rupee note, c. 1930, showing King George VI and a post-independence Indian Rupee note, c. 1990, with British royalty replaced with an image of the Lion Capital at Sarnath, a monument erected c. 250 BCE by the early Indian emperor Ashoka.

Money lets us keep records.

On a tablet from ancient Mesopotamia, anthropologists uncovered notes of debts, paid labor, and beer, grain, and animals that were exchanged. And of course, businesses use money to figure out their financial status.

Money helps us teach our children.

Our attitudes about money begin at home. A child's allowance is much more than an amount and can be used by parents to teach important life lessons.

Putting all of this together, we have global power, national authority, local values, and family lessons. We see how money is woven through the fabric of our obligations and recordkeeping.

Bitcoin

We also wind up with a group of people who were very dissatisfied with money. Saying they wanted to eliminate the power that central authorities have over money, they created digital currencies over which no central bank had power.

First described in 2008 and created in 2009, Bitcoin's origins are somewhat obscure. While Satoshi Nakamoto created it, no one knows who Satoshi Nakamoto is—or whether he or she exists, and if they are one person or many. We are told that no more than 21 million Bitcoin can be issued. We also know that accessing new Bitcoin requires a "mining" process that involves massive computing power.

It is likely that once you receive your Bitcoin, you will store it in a digital wallet. When you do, make sure you remember the wallet's password. If you lose it, you will not be able to access your Bitcoin. Ever. Forgetful individuals have lost millions.

Although Bitcoin took us to the closing pages of this chapter, it could be just the beginning of how money will work in a digital society—and signal a return to a cashless world.

Continuing to look at the circular flow model, our lens now will focus on what we measure. Only through our yardsticks can we evaluate fiscal and monetary policies. The big question, though, is deciding what to measure. Through GDP we have some answers and more questions.

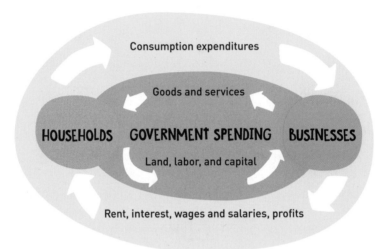

THE FIRST GDP

Our story starts in 1665, with an official who wanted to prove Great Britain could afford a war against Holland and France. By estimating the size of national income, spending, and other assets (which no one previously knew), William Petty confirmed there was sufficient tax revenue and land, labor, and capital to fight the Second Anglo-Dutch War (1664–1667). Unknowingly, he had calculated Gross Domestic Product (GDP).

Fast forwarding, we can look at the 1930s for the true beginning of modern GDP computation. When economic activity shrunk and joblessness climbed, no one knew precisely what had happened or why. Only by learning that the national income—how much we pay ourselves for everything we produce—had gone down by one half between 1929 and 1932 could the US president plan his recovery program. Searching for similar information, in Britain John Maynard Keynes explained that he needed to know much more about what the UK economy could produce when he wrote *How to Pay for the War* (1940). As he complained, governments "regarded the collection of essential facts as a waste of money." Increasingly agreeing with Keynes, nations soon realized they needed to know the numbers in order to fight the Great Depression and World War II. In the UK, as early as the 1920s, we can see the quarterly income data the government began to collect. As a result, by 1930, Great Britain set up the National Economic Advisory Council to interpret and advise on the data it gathered.

Similarly, across the ocean, the US had Simon Kuznets leading the statistical attack. Destined to become a Nobel laureate, Kuznets shaped the earliest GDP identity that let us know the money value of the goods and services produced by the economy. Wanting no "dis-services" in his production totals, he excluded illegal goods and services and even military armament. Home production was not included, either, as it was not possible to assign a market price to activities such as housework. Consequently, if you did your own cooking it was not counted in national income totals. But if you hired a chef, her salary was included.

Unemployed men queue outside a soup kitchen in Chicago during the Great Depression.

Even government activity was left out of the first national income totals. But soon statisticians decided that a submarine purchase or a judge's salary is a new good or a service whose production we need to record. After all, when the state purchases a submarine or pays the salary of a judge, the cost has to be recorded and the service it supplies accounted for.

In the following pages, to see how GDP has evolved, we will consider what it comprises—from its numbers to its human dimension. We will also look at how we calculate GDP and whether it should change.

CALCULATING GDP
Three Approaches

GDP as we understand it today is the descendant of Simon Kuznets's national accounting concept. It's the Gross Domestic Product because it covers what is made inside a country. Until 1991, nations used the GNP—Gross National Product. Somewhat different from the domestic focus of GDP, a nation's GNP covered all items made by that country's companies around the world.

There are three different approaches we can use to calculate GDP, but whichever one we use brings us to the same totals. In the upper loop of our circular flow model, we can see what we spend on goods and services through the expenditures approach. Then the incomes we pay to produce them, or the value they gather as their production unfolds, occupy the lower loop.

Three GDP Methods		
Expenditures (What we spend)	• Spending from households, businesses, and government • Exports (made domestically, minus imports made elsewhere)	Hypothetical total 100
Incomes (What we pay ourselves)	• Wages and salaries • Profit and proprietors' income • Rent • Interest • Dividends	Hypothetical total 100
Output (What we produce)	• Total output less change in inventories minus intermediate inputs (the items used to make the final good, such as energy and raw materials)	Hypothetical total 100

The three GDP approaches take us to what we spend, what we pay ourselves, and what things are worth. They also let us connect the upper loop GDP to our lower loop National Income by moving from GDP to NDP (Net Domestic Product) to NI (National Income). To make the journey, we need to just subtract depreciation from GDP to arrive at the NDP. As the difference between GDP and NDP, depreciation represents equipment that has "worn out." It is a car that has been driven, or an older refrigeration unit in a supermarket that is not quite as cold as it was when it was first installed. We could say that subtracting what has disappeared from capital gives us a more accurate investment number. And then, by again doing some subtracting but this time for indirect business taxes, we arrive at the NI. Indirect business taxes could be sales taxes, VAT (value added taxes) or any other tax that comes from a different payer, rather than directly from the business.

GROSS NATIONAL PRODUCT (GNP) ▶ *the money value of the final goods and services produced by a country within and beyond its borders during a specific time period (usually a year).*

NET DOMESTIC PRODUCT (NDP) ▶ *GDP minus depreciation (also known as capital consumption), the process through which used capital becomes less valuable.*

NET INVESTMENT ▶ *gross investment minus depreciation.*

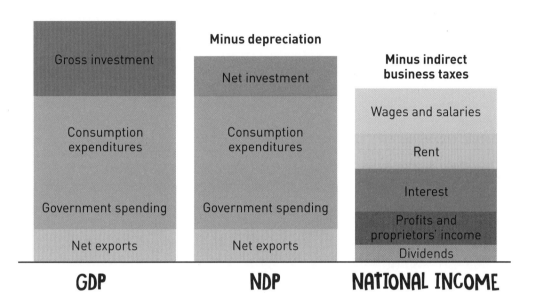

Returning to our circular flow model, above, the first two columns represent the upper loop while the national income is the lower loop.

DEPRECIATION ▶ *when, over time, a capital good loses some value.*
The difference between GDP and NDP.

The Expenditures Approach

Taking a closer look at the expenditures approach, we see four GDP components:

- C: consumption
- I: gross investment
- G: government
- Net exports: international trade.

More than half of the US, the UK, and other high-income countries' GDPs, consumption expenditures (or household consumption) include the prices of the goods and services that you and I, as consumers, might buy. Then, depending on whether they last for more or less than three years, the goods part of C is divided into durables and non-durables. Thus washing machines and refrigerators are classified as durable goods while, more short-lived, a latte and perhaps a t-shirt are non-durables.

Then, to complete the consumption component, we need to add the intangible items an economy produces. Ranging from piano lessons to dental examinations, they are easy to quantify when they have a price. However, we shall see shortly why very intangible services, for example using Google Search, create massive GDP headaches.

CONSUMPTION ▶ *the GDP component that totals the money value of the goods and services that households use.*

DURABLE AND NON-DURABLE GOODS ▶ *the goods we produce that have an average life of more than three years are called durable; those we expect to last for fewer than three years are our non-durables.*

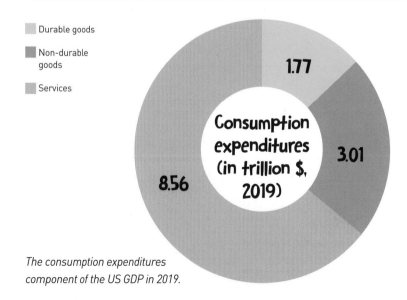

- Durable goods
- Non-durable goods
- Services

1.77

3.01

8.56

Consumption expenditures (in trillion $, 2019)

The consumption expenditures component of the US GDP in 2019.

Next, remaining in the private sector, gross investment takes us to businesses… but not entirely. In addition to the tools and equipment that are in our investment slice, we have residential housing and "change in inventory." As you might expect, residential housing represents the value of the new structures consumers can purchase. Also, though, statisticians needed a "change in inventory" number to avoid double counting. For example, imagine that Starbucks does not sell a new mug during an entire year. Unsold, it becomes inventory and adds an extra $3 to GDP for that year. Then, however, assume it is sold during the following year. Consequently, it gets added to C and subtracted from inventory, thereby becoming a "zero" for that second year.

And thirdly, as our last "plus" category, we have government spending on goods and services. We need to be sure, though, that government payments are for what we make. Not a part of the GDP, transfer payments such as a UK state pension deposit or a US Social Security check received by a 68-year-old retiree reflect nothing that has been produced. Consequently, transfer payments are not counted in GDP.

GROSS INVESTMENT ▶ the GDP component whose main parts are the money values of business expenditures on new plants, equipment, software, and also residential housing. Smaller items include research and development and change in inventories.

TRANSFER PAYMENTS ▶ government payments (including the UK state pension and US Social Security) that do not represent the creation of a good or a service.

Net exports (exports minus imports)

Finally, since we are recording all domestic production, we have to include what leaves the country (X) and exclude what comes in (M). Recognizing that the value of imports usually exceeds what exports are worth, we add a negative number for net exports to GDP for this component.

GDP totals

To see how to calculate GDP, we can return to Starbucks. Massively oversimplifying, we can figure out its contribution to the GDP with C+I+G+(X-M). We just need to add a latte (C) to the coffee machine (I) to the neighborhood police officer (G) and subtract the coffee beans (net exports).

Using very hypothetical numbers, assume C is $10, I is $4, G is $5, and net exports is negative $3, because the beans came from beyond our borders. As a result, Starbucks added $16 to GDP.

Strolling around the upper loop of a circular flow model, we can observe all of the C+I+G+(X-M) transactions. Next, taking us to the circular flow's lower loop, statisticians use incomes to determine their GDP totals. They add together the wages and salaries, rent, interest, and profits that we pay ourselves. Then, through the third way, they total the value added at the different stages of producing goods and services. For a pretzel, they could start with the wheat on the farm and conclude with a manufacturer and a supermarket.

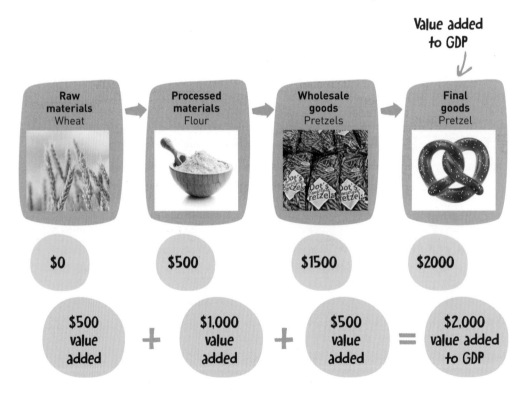

CALCULATING ECONOMIC GROWTH

Our final goal—and the one number that is crucial for assessing fiscal and monetary policy—is economic growth. To generate more affluence, to elevate standards of living, and to accommodate an increasing population, economies need to grow.

Real and Nominal GDP

First, however, we have a problem.

When inflation boosts prices, the numbers are misleading. For example, if, in year one, the price of an orange was $1, and we produced three, the $3 gets added to the GDP. Then, during year two, because of inflation, assume the price rises to $1.25. So, for three oranges, we would have added $3.75 to what is called the nominal GDP. The nominal GDP records current numbers. Yes, it could appear that the economy grew. But it did not.

Instead, we need to calculate real GDP by selecting what we call a base year. Base years just give us a reference point for converting money into its spending power for that year. Then, converting nominal GDP into real GDP, we can compare our numbers.

Real GDP in Year 1 = (nominal GDP x 100)/price index

The price index to which we are referring is a basket of goods that serve as our barometer of price changes. It could be a Consumer Price Index in the US or the Retail Prices Index (RPI) in the UK. It could include or exclude mortgage costs or impute a rental price for your dwelling. In August 2022, the UK's CPI at 9.9 percent was less than the RPI's 12.3 percent. Whichever a country selects, the key for us is that it takes you from nominal to real. It prevents inflation from being misleading.

Then, finally, we can follow the countless pathways to the growth rate. But, basically, we are comparing the current real GDP to a past real GDP. To calculate the economic growth rate, this is one possible fraction.

$$\text{ECONOMIC GROWTH RATE} = \frac{\text{end (GDP) minus beginning (GDP)}}{\text{beginning (GPD)}} \times 100$$

Per Capita GDP

In addition to the aggregate, we can ask if growth kept up with an increase in population. Called per capita GDP, we just divide GDP by population and then calculate per capita GDP growth rates.

THE BUSINESS CYCLE

At this point, we should note that growth does not move steadily upward. Instead, we have a business cycle with four phases. We have an expansionary phase when production increases. Then as those totals climb more slowly, we touch a peak before the contraction begins. A descending growth rate and then a decline take us to a trough—the absolute bottom. Here, the expansion resumes. With firms hiring and people spending more, GDP gets increasingly bigger—more than previously—until it hits a peak. And from there we start the slide downward again.

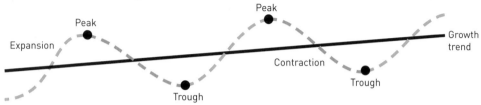

BUSINESS CYCLE ▶ *composed of an expansionary period, a peak, a contraction, and then a trough, the business cycle displays the ups and downs of an economy.*

Recession

During a business cycle contraction, we could have a recession. In the US, for example, when the NBER (National Bureau of Economic Research) or the NIESR (National Institute of Economic and Social Research) identify two successive quarters of a declining GDP, they will say that the US is in recession. Also, though, they need to see that other indicators such as employment and consumption expenditures are slumping. Looking at the "depth, diffusion, and/or duration" of the decline, they can say when it began and when it ended. As a result, they quantify the path of the business cycle.

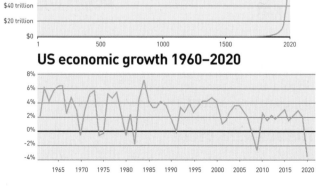

So, yes, in a single number, the GDP is supposed to tell us the total value of the final goods and services that a nation produces in a year. From there, we can decide if the economy is growing. And then we can decide the appropriate fiscal and monetary policy response.

But we know that it is not always that simple.

US unemployment rate

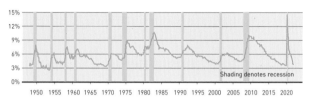

THE HUMAN SIDE OF GDP

Quantitative and seemingly impersonal, GDP has a human side that impacts countless lives through the goods and services the numbers represent at home and at work.

At Home

If you visited the home of a typical housewife at the beginning of the 20th century, you would have seen her spending approximately seven hours a week doing the family wash. In addition to hauling and boiling thousands of gallons of water in her home, dirty clothes needed scrubbing, washing, wringing, and drying. Washing machines became commercially available from the 1930s, and if our typical housewife had found herself in possession of one, she could have used the time it saved her to read or write more, or join the labor force. Considered from the human angle, the addition of the washing machine to GDP represented the time and energy she saved and the productivity she added.

Somewhat similarly, during the 20th century we would have seen the spread of electrification, flush toilets, air conditioners, cars, and refrigerators. Diets became more nutritious, homes had more bedrooms, people's health improved. Furthermore, because of the increasing use of the automobile, road networks grew, and even fast food outlets like McDonald's sprang up at seemingly every intersection.

At Work

At the same time, manufacturing efficiency was transformed. The way that books are produced illustrates this perfectly. Rewinding to the Middle Ages, scribes laboring over manuscripts could produce an estimated 3,000 words of plain text each day. At this rate, it took 136 days to make one bible. Realizing there had to be a better, more efficient way, Johannes Gutenberg invented the printing press. It was an adapted wine press and sped up the bible production process from one book every 136 days to 340 books in the same period (or 2.5 books each day). Today, with little cost and time at the margin, through online book "production" manufacturers offer potentially infinite print runs.

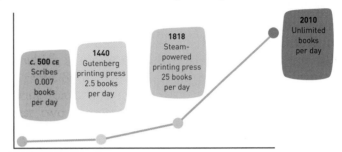

INCREASING RETURNS TO SCALE ▶ *when less or the same input creates more output because of the synergy between mass production and technological progress.*

Shown by books but applicable to countless items, the increasing returns to scale—more output from less or the same input—created by the synergy between mass production and technological progress also boosted GDP totals.

EVALUATING GDP

All of this takes us to a final question. By measuring the value of the goods and services that we produce, we elevate its importance. Although, inevitably, we will "treasure what we measure," perhaps we need to reconsider what we count.

Uncounted Items

We can first ask what needs to be included. In 2014, when the European Union tightened its requirement that nations recognize excluded items from the "shadow economy" in their GDP, newly added estimates of sex industry and drug trade transactions inflated Spain's GDP by an extra 1 percent. The most notable surge, though, had already occurred. In 1987, after adding black market activity to its GDP, Italy suddenly became the world's fifth-largest economy. Further complicating GDP comparisons, we had the US expanding its investment component by adding items such as research and development (R&D) in 2013. By also including R&D as a final good rather than an intermediate item, the EU boosted its GDP by 3.5 percent.

SHADOW ECONOMY ▶ *activities excluded from GDP that are typically all or partially illegal because cash payments are not reported.*

Production or Well-Being

We can also ask if we want GDP to quantify production or well-being. Either, however, is problematic because the original GDP was meant to measure the elements of what was mostly a manufacturing economy. Consequently, it inadequately recognizes the massive impact of the internet. Whether considering production or well-being, we have a huge disconnect.

Misleading Prices

We need to ask what to count when price is zero. For example, we receive a service when an app on our phone steers us away from a traffic jam. Assuming we did not pay for the app and presumably used less gas by avoiding the problems on the road, GDP was lower than it would have been. Similarly, decades ago, most families owned a set of encyclopedias; now we use our Wikis. You can see where this is going. There are so many goods and services today that we do not pay for that are produced (adding to output) and that improve our lives (adding to well-being).

GDP also has the challenge of accurately quantifying vastly improved products. Replacing disruptive and lengthy medical procedures, minimally invasive surgery can be cheaper and require less hospital time. It too can tug GDP downward.

Externalities

To this long list, we cannot forget the "disservices" that add to GDP. Increased air pollution can create more asthma, extra visits to the doctor, and a higher GDP.

A GDP Commission

Worried about GDP deficiencies, the former French president Nicolas Sarkozy asked Nobel laureate Joseph Stiglitz to lead a GDP inquiry. As the Stiglitz Commission on the Measurement of Economic Performance and Social Progress expressed, "What we measure affects what we do; and if our measurements are flawed, decisions may be distorted."

One of the main conclusions of the commission's report was that our task was to shift our emphasis from output to well-being. Consequently, GDP needed to focus on household income and on what different income groups spend. Their well-being list began with material living standards, moved on to health, education, and political voice, and concluded with "insecurity" and environmental sustainability. For each new variable they suggested creating a robust metric.

Fiscal and Monetary Policy

At this point, we can return to where we began. Knowing the numbers, we theoretically should be able to guide fiscal and monetary policy more wisely. With more government spending, lower taxes, and lower interest rates, we should be able to stimulate the economic activity that moves around our circular flow model. By contrast, the opposite should be true when we constrain economic activity with less spending, higher taxes, and higher interest rates.

However, we have not perfectly worked this out. Sometimes, when we stimulate economic activity and reduce unemployment, we get more inflation than we expected. Then, to moderate inflation, we boost unemployment, and perhaps create another problem.

The trade-off between inflation and unemployment has been illustrated by a Phillips Curve. More recently, having flattened, the trade-off is debatable.

So yes, we do know more about how to diagnose our economic illnesses and what their cures are. As with all cures, though, we cannot guarantee that they will work. But, by keeping track, we can better understand the present and plan for the future.

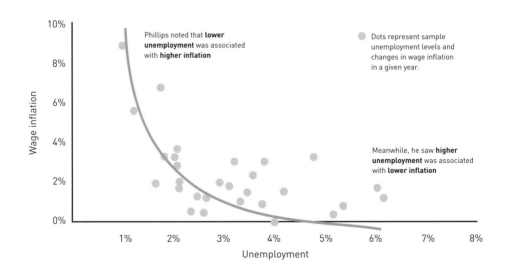

Chapter Nine
THE FINANCIAL SYSTEM

The Crash—The 1930s—
Commercial and Investment Banks—
Regulation—Securities Markets—
The Impact of Technology—
Economic Policy

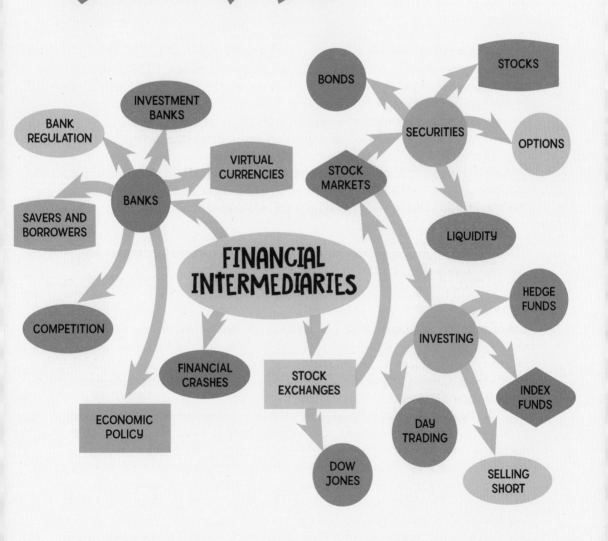

BONDS

STOCKS

INVESTMENT
BANKS

SECURITIES

OPTIONS

BANK
REGULATION

VIRTUAL
CURRENCIES

STOCK
MARKETS

BANKS

SAVERS AND
BORROWERS

LIQUIDITY

FINANCIAL
INTERMEDIARIES

HEDGE
FUNDS

INVESTING

COMPETITION

INDEX
FUNDS

FINANCIAL
CRASHES

STOCK
EXCHANGES

DAY
TRADING

ECONOMIC
POLICY

DOW
JONES

SELLING
SHORT

Rather like the human heart, a state's financial system pumps the money and the credit that sustain the life of the economy. This money and credit flow through the banks and securities markets that connect the people who save money to those who want to borrow and/or invest it.

THE CRASH

Our story starts in 1929, when stock markets crashed, banks failed, and countries defaulted on the bonds they had sold. Worried, depositors rushed to banks to withdraw their savings. But because one person's deposit had become someone else's business loan or home mortgage, the money wasn't there.

This was not a new phenomenon. Faced with distressed borrowers and concerned depositors, bank failures had multiplied between 1921 and 1929. This culminated in what became known as Black Tuesday, October 29, 1929, when prices collapsed on the New York Stock Exchange and the Great Depression began. It would last a decade and few, if any, countries around the world were unaffected by it—although its effects were particularly debilitating in the US and in Europe.

Much later, in 2022, a Nobel Prize winner—Benjamin Bernanke—described the importance of banks. But first, our stroll around the circular flow will take us to commercial and investment banks and securities markets.

SECURITIES ▶ *including stock and bonds, financial instruments we can buy and sell that represent value.*

THE 1930s

Recognizing the financial crisis as a threat to the entire economy, the US Senate's Committee on Banking and Currency scheduled a series of hearings to identify the problem and its possible solutions. J.P. Morgan Jr., son of the world's most famous banker and the head of his namesake company, was among the people they called to testify.

J.P. Morgan & Co. was founded in 1871 and grew to be a global banking and financial empire. As a commercial and investment bank, it funded wealthy individuals and large corporations. John Pierpont Morgan controlled the organization until his death in 1913, overseeing the expansion of an entire capital goods sector of the US economy, and helping to create the securities that funded industries ranging from steel to electricity. He also directed the reorganization of the railroads when the industry collapsed in the early 1890s, and resolved a banking panic in 1907—all from the comfort of his library.

A circular flow and financial intermediaries

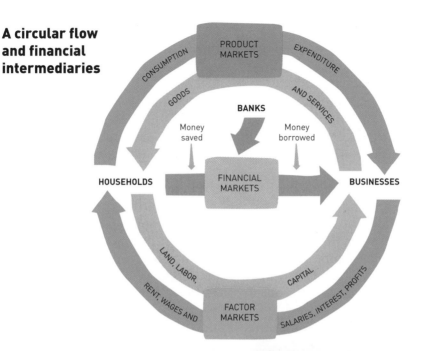

As a financial intermediary, J.P. Morgan & Co. was the conduit through which money moved. A home for deposits and a source of loans, as a commercial bank it serviced an affluent clientele. Correspondingly, for many of the same people, J.P. Morgan also served as an investment bank that originated and sold stocks and bonds.

J.P. Morgan was a large, striking man, whose distinguishing feature was a large, red, bulbous nose. It may have been the result of a medical condition that also left him with rosacea (a skin condition) and which made him prone to headaches and fainting spells.

FINANCIAL INTERMEDIARY ▶ *a firm that connects savers and borrowers.*

By the time of Morgan's death, the US banking sector was beginning to change. The government was increasingly taking a role in—and control of—the economy. In 1933, when J.P. Morgan Jr. appeared before a Senate inquiry into suspect banking practices—an indignity, perhaps, his immensely powerful father would never have suffered. Worse was to follow, however. After one of the senators at the inquiry had described the proceedings as a circus, an enterprising journalist arranged for a 27-inch-tall circus performer to be brought into the inquiry and she was photographed sitting on a rather bemused J.P. Morgan Jr.'s lap. It is impossible to imagine J.P. Morgan Sr. allowing himself to become the subject of such a publicity stunt.

In some ways, this incident symbolizes the decline in influence of America's banking sector in this period, as controls and investigations were introduced to regulate it. Once the Great Depression was over, banking and institutions would never be the same again—not just in the US but around the world.

BOND ▶ *a debt obligation from a government or a business firm. Bonds typically pay interest and have a maturity date when the loan is repaid.*

COMMERCIAL AND INVESTMENT BANKS

In the Glass-Steagall Banking Act of 1933, the US Congress established deposit insurance and eliminated the conflicts of interest that let bankers use depositors' funds for risky investments. They said that no longer could firms like J.P. Morgan fund business expansion and development with deposits. Instead, like all other similar financial intermediaries, J.P. Morgan & Co. would be divided into a commercial bank and an investment bank to become two separate firms.

Whether a commercial bank, an investment bank, or both, today's banks pump money and credit around our economy. Like J.P. Morgan's financial intermediation, they connect savers and borrowers.

Commercial Banks

Households and businesses are typical commercial bank customers. The banks' liabilities come from the depositors that trust them with their money, while their assets are the loans for businesses and residential housing.

COMMERCIAL BANK ▶ *a financial intermediary that connects savers and borrowers through pools of savings created by deposits and loans to businesses and households.*

Commercial banks
fuel economic activity through the money they combine and the information they generate

Pools of savings
Because banks, as depository institutions, create pools of savings, they can make large and small loans to many individuals and businesses.

Multiple borrowers
By having more borrowers, banks can reduce their risk.

Sources of information
When banks research the creditworthiness of potential borrowers, they solve problems that relate to "information asymmetry."

Through their quest for the profits that interest payments on loans bring them, banks have to examine who is risk worthy. The answers, shown in financial markets, determine who does and does not get a loan, as well as how much interest the person or business pays.

Always, though, as financial intermediaries, commercial bankers match savers and borrowers.

INFORMATION ASYMMETRY ▶ *a transactional situation in which one party knows more than the other(s) about the details of that transaction and its background.*

NATIONAL INCOME SAVING RATES, 2021

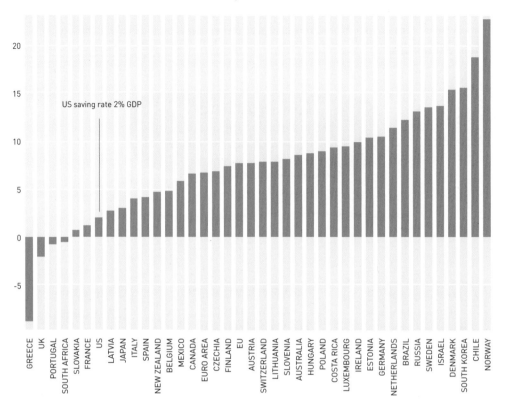

US saving rate 2% GDP

Investment Banks

Investment banks focus on the business sector of the circular flow model. As financial intermediaries, they match savers and borrowers through the securities they produce and distribute. With the IOUs we call bonds, they facilitate the loans for businesses and municipalities that could be the smallest towns or the largest nations. If a large nation or a small municipality wants to build a bridge (or spend money on countless other projects), it usually goes to the fixed income people at investment banks. They are called "fixed income" because the interest paid by a bond is usually established when the bond is issued. Those fixed income people determine the details of the security they will create. They need to decide the bond's interest rate and its payback maturity date. It is also possible to sell bonds before they mature if the previous owners pass the contractual obligations to a new bondholder.

INVESTMENT BANK ▶ *a financial intermediary that connects savers and borrowers by enabling individuals, businesses, and municipalities to provide and access money through securities.*

Borrowing through bonds and providing financial knowhow, investment bankers help to fuel the circular flow's economic activity:

1. Pools of IOUs: Similar to bank loans, bond markets spread risk. Rather than placing all of their eggs in one basket, the investors that buy these IOUs have a vast array of choices that lets them diversify.
2. Liquidity: Bond markets create liquidity—the availability of cash—because bond owners can sell a security before it matures.

REGULATION

The indispensable role played by banks has made regulators wonder if they should let them compete. Knowing that the entire economy could be jeopardized by a bank's risky behavior, regulators impose a series of rules to govern how banks operate. While these regulations vary from country to country, they all aim to protect the wider economy from bank failures and to ensure that the financial system continues to function effectively. To understand the role played by regulation better, we will take a closer a look at its evolution in the United States.

After the crisis caused by the Wall Street Crash of 1929, regulators in the 1930s said "No" to the unregulated free-for-all that had preceded it. When circumstances changed 40 years later, they had a new answer. Then, they switched again in 2010.

In 1933, responding to hundreds of bank failures and the fragility of the financial system, the US Congress passed the landmark Glass-Steagall Banking Act that forced banks to split themselves into commercial and investment institutions. J.P. Morgan & Co, for example, was divided into a commercial bank (J.P. Morgan) and an investment bank (Morgan Stanley). By separating financial institutions in this way, Congress sought to minimize banks' risky behavior. In addition, to prevent the bank runs that create bank failures, Congress established deposit guarantees with the Federal Deposit Insurance Corporation (FDIC). Through Glass-Steagall and other regulations that prohibited banks from establishing interstate branches and limited the interest they could pay depositors, banking activities were constrained.

The office of J.P. Morgan, c. 1906.

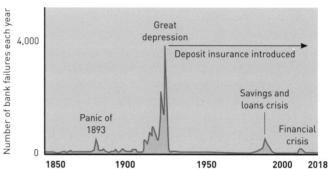

After touching a high during the 1920s and 1930s, US bank failures became rather rare. You can see the inverse correlation between the failures and deposit insurance.

Carter Glass and Henry Steagall.

It all worked ideally for more than 40 years. Conservatively run, banks rarely experienced the bank runs and failures that had become all too common in the 1920s and early 1930s. But then a problem developed. With interest rates capped, banks could not compete against other institutions that started to capture their customers with a new, more lucrative financial product called the money market fund. The money they raised was mostly used to buy US government securities. Almost as safe as insured accounts, the new kind of fund offered returns that were significantly higher than the paltry amounts permitted on savings deposits. The result was disintermediation—a term indicating the banks were doing less financial intermediation because depositors were going elsewhere. Realizing they had to inject some life into the industry, regulators

The UK bank Northern Rock failed after a run in 2007.

decided that US banks should be allowed to expand beyond state lines, offer more interest to savers, and have investment banking subsidiaries. Long before Glass-Steagall was formally repealed in 1999, individual financial institutions had begun to engage in commercial and investment activities.

The results were predictable. Having fewer regulatory restraints, banks helped to create a global financial crisis in the first decade of the 21st century. This time, they bought risky securities that became worthless when housing markets collapsed. As in the 1920s, monetary officials around the world began to worry that they would experience a cascade of bank failures.

In the US, the immediate response was the central bank's purchase of those worthless securities. In short, a bailout. As Chair of the Federal Reserve, Ben Bernanke had hoped that, by boosting banks' balance sheets, he could encourage the banks that were avoiding risk to restart lending.

The biggest worry, though, was a system collapse. Regulators wanted to avoid the 19th-century solution when markets had eliminated the weaker banks because the cost had been banking panics and economic depressions. Instead, by identifying the financial institutions that were "too big to fail," they could prevent the catastrophic impact of a systemic collapse. However, if a bank knows it will be preserved, it has the incentive to engage in risky behavior. Called moral hazard, the downside of systemic protection is that it encourages more risk.

MORAL HAZARD ▶ *an attitude that is created when the downside of risk is minimized, thereby creating the incentive to take on more risk.*

As explained by Ben Bernanke, one of the recipients of the 2022 Nobel Memorial Prize in Economics, systemic protection is crucial because it can preclude a contractionary credit ripple where banks lend less. When economic activity declines, the value of the collateral a borrower uses also decreases. As a result, banks offer fewer loans and we have what has been called the "progressive erosion of borrowers' collateral." Having fewer good borrowers increasingly shrinks economic activity. Recognizing that a downward borrowing spiral helped to intensify and lengthen the Great Depression of the 1930s, contemporary economists advocated the regulatory vigilance that would preserve lending.

One result was the Dodd-Frank Wall Street Reform and Consumer Protection Act of 2010. Although the Act was admired for the consumer protections it introduced, it was also condemned for its complexity. By 2014, and still not fully implemented, the Act numbered almost 14,000 pages. That said, its rationale could be summarized into two key goals:

- Minimize the risks that financial institutions had taken.
- Protect consumers from unwise financial decisions.

To achieve these goals, the Act had four main sections that regulatory agencies were supposed to populate with specific guidelines.

A satire on the "tulipomania" of 1637 by Jan Brueghel the Younger.

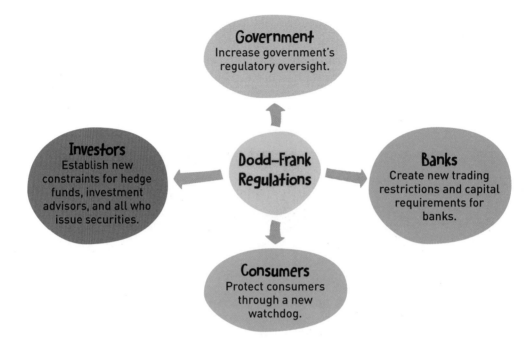

Somewhat similar to the US's cure for its banking ailments, the UK passed the Banking Reform Act in 2013. Meanwhile, in the EU, the goal was a banking union. As of 2022, EU members were still working on an agreement. One sticking point was deposit insurance. Like the debate in the US during the 1930s, the robust banks worried they would carry the burden for everyone else. They had made progress, though, by creating the "Single Supervisory Mechanism" for all EU banks and identifying a set of wind-down rules for troubled financial institutions.

SECURITIES MARKETS

At this point, our story of commercial and investment banking needs one more component to make it complete. It needs a third financial intermediary that is closely related to banks. And then we need to see how the three relate to each other. Like banks, securities markets are a financial link. They connect people who have money to the individuals and institutions that will invest it. And as we did with banking, let's begin with a look at the past.

In 1602, after the last of its original shares of ownership were sold, trading in the Dutch East India Company commenced. As both buyers and sellers needed a place where they could find each other, they started to meet by one of Amsterdam's many bridges. Amsterdam is not the world's warmest or driest city, so traders decided to take their business indoors—and built for themselves the first stock exchange. Completed in 1611, it was mainly where commodities such as beer, salt, grain, and timber were traded. In the rear section of the structure, investors exchanged shares (which resembled bonds), expecting to profit from the spices that Dutch East India Company vessels brought home from the Orient.

Somewhat similarly, the market on Wall Street in the 1790s was primarily composed of dealers, brokers, and auctioneers. The dealers typically bought and sold securities for their own accounts; brokers had customers for whom they traded; auctioneers were the middlemen, offering securities for sale to the highest bidder. Taking the next step, 24 of the people who had been trading at 68 Wall Street under a buttonwood tree signed an agreement that prevented outsiders from participating in their auctions. Called the Buttonwood Agreement, it described how they auctioned securities, which securities they selected, and who could purchase their services. Although contemporary historians question the direct connection, they do conclude that the Buttonwood Group was a seed from which the New York Stock Exchange eventually grew.

Explaining the Market

When we hear the word "market" it's natural to think of it as a physical space. It could be a supermarket, a flower market, or a farmer's market, each with items for sale, buyers in the aisles, and sellers hoping to convince them to make purchases. At cash registers people pay the marked price or haggle until they agree a new price. Also the location of a market, the NY Stock Exchange building is at 11 Wall Street.

HEDGE FUND ▶ *an actively-managed financial fund that offsets potential losses through investing in a variety of different assets.*

We know, however, that markets do not have to be located at a specific site. When there are items for sale, and buyers, sellers, and prices that people are willing and able to pay, a market exists. In contemporary securities markets, stocks, bonds, and less tangible options or derivatives and other representations of financial value are the items for sale. Online and in person, securities markets are systems through which savers and investors interact.

This buttonwood tree was toppled by a storm on June 14, 1865.

OPTION ▶ *a contract that gives the buyer the right to purchase or sell different kinds of securities at another time for a pre-determined price.*

STOCK ▶ *representations of shares of ownership of a corporation. One person, many people, and businesses can own all, some, or a small proportion of the shares of a corporation.*

DERIVATIVE ▶ *a security whose value is based on other securities.*

Representing ownership in a corporation, stock is one of the many types of securities. If that ownership has been divided into 100 shares of stock, then the person who sells one share is transferring a 1/100th ownership portion of that business to someone else. Vastly oversimplifying stock market basics, we can look at orders to buy at certain prices on the demand side; then, also, we have sellers with their price preferences on the supply side. In our hypothetical market, when there are more buy orders than sell orders, price goes up. If there is more for sale than people want to buy, the opposite occurs. No one dictates what price should be. No one says how much should be bought and sold. In markets, following the laws of demand and supply, prices are determined.

Benefits

Although stock markets differ, all convey some of the same benefits. Like banks, they propel money around the circular flow.

The markets through which shares of stock are bought and sold exist in countless ways. You might ask a stockbroker or financial advisor to carry out a securities transaction. As a result, they could submit the order to the London Stock Exchange or to Nasdaq, a market that is dominated by tech stocks. They can trade through the New York Stock Exchange, the Mongolian Stock Exchange, or any stock exchange anywhere in the world. It would all depend on the market (or markets) through which a company trades.

It is also possible that the seller of a large block of shares contacts a potential buyer directly. We have high frequency trading in which my computer "talks" to your computer. We have Index Funds. There are day traders, individuals

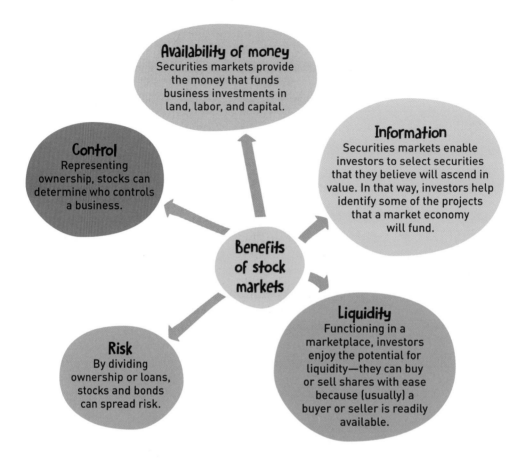

Availability of money
Securities markets provide the money that funds business investments in land, labor, and capital.

Information
Securities markets enable investors to select securities that they believe will ascend in value. In that way, investors help identify some of the projects that a market economy will fund.

Control
Representing ownership, stocks can determine who controls a business.

Benefits of stock markets

Liquidity
Functioning in a marketplace, investors enjoy the potential for liquidity—they can buy or sell shares with ease because (usually) a buyer or seller is readily available.

Risk
By dividing ownership or loans, stocks and bonds can spread risk.

who hold stocks for many years, and people called market makers who, yes, make markets for a specific security. Through Initial Public Offerings (IPOs), investment bankers create, price, and then sell new shares of a company's stock to us. So the list of market participants and trading vehicles is long and changing daily.

But there is more.

You have to decide if your investing will depend on the stock going up or down. More traditionally, we try to buy low and then sell high. However, the market also has its "short sellers" that want stock prices to decrease. When you sell short, first you borrow stock and then you sell it. Next you wait for the price to sink, and, when it does, you buy the stock. Lastly, you return what you borrowed. As you can see, first you sold high and then you bought low. Since selling short depends on the stock price going down, you will have major problems if the price rises because you have to return what you borrowed.

SELLING SHORT ▶ *an investing style that is successful when price goes down because investors first sell borrowed stock, wait for the price to decrease, then buy the stock, and return what they borrowed.*

Meanwhile, investment bankers can participate in securities markets to buy and sell the bonds they create. Whereas the amount many bonds pay to their holders is a constant, through markets the rates can fluctuate, based on their current purchase price. Still, there are a slew of interest rate scenarios. Some float, some are fixed, and some, known as zero coupon bonds, provide no interest. Beyond all of this, we have bond-like securities that, for example, are backed by bundles of mortgages.

Further complicating the picture but not nearly completing it, we can see what institutional investors do. Defined as the larger investors such as pension funds, insurance companies, and mutual funds, institutional investors buy larger blocks of securities. The mortgages we buy, for example, to finance a house purchase are combined into bundles of loans which become a security that an institutional investor buys.

INDEX FUND ▶ *a financial fund that is composed of many securities, usually from a certain category. Index funds track market indices like the S&P 500 by owning some or all of the securities in that index.*

MUTUAL FUND ▶ *an investing vehicle that makes shares of a diverse portfolio available to small and large buyers.*

Whether it's Amsterdam, Wall Street, or Mongolia, wherever securities trade, one thread connects them. When the owners of commodities or bonds or shares of companies or the initiators of new ventures sought money, they needed to know where to go. Their destination was a securities market.

Other Stock Markets

In the developing world, in 2016, Lesotho's central bank launched its first stock exchange and, in 2021, got its first listing. Meanwhile, Egypt has had a stock market since 1883. More recently, stock markets were established in Saudi Arabia (1984), Iceland (1985), and Laos (2011). Many appeared in Eastern Europe from the 1990s onwards.

With capitalization referring to the total money value of all securities, we see the US, China, Japan, and Hong Kong are where companies listed by stock markets have the highest dollar value.

Looking at the location of the largest stock exchanges, we see China is the only middle-income nation among all of the others that are more developed.

ALL STOCKS' CAPITALIZATION AROUND THE WORLD

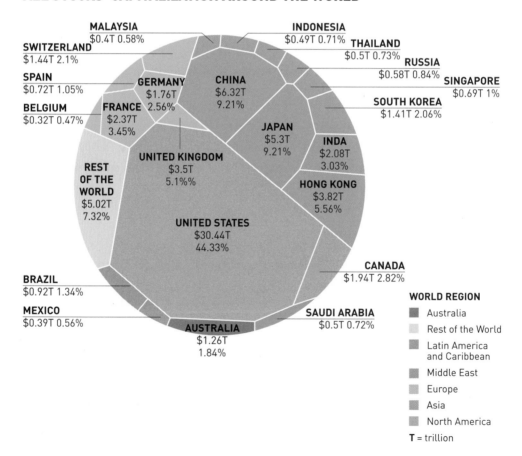

MALAYSIA
$0.4T 0.58%

SWITZERLAND
$1.44T 2.1%

SPAIN
$0.72T 1.05%

BELGIUM
$0.32T 0.47%

GERMANY
$1.76T 2.56%

FRANCE
$2.37T
3.45%

CHINA
$6.32T
9.21%

INDONESIA
$0.49T 0.71%

THAILAND
$0.5T 0.73%

RUSSIA
$0.58T 0.84%

SINGAPORE
$0.69T 1%

SOUTH KOREA
$1.41T 2.06%

JAPAN
$5.3T
9.21%

INDA
$2.08T
3.03%

REST
OF THE
WORLD
$5.02T
7.32%

UNITED KINGDOM
$3.5T
5.1%%

HONG KONG
$3.82T
5.56%

UNITED STATES
$30.44T
44.33%

BRAZIL
$0.92T 1.34%

MEXICO
$0.39T 0.56%

CANADA
$1.94T 2.82%

AUSTRALIA
$1.26T
1.84%

SAUDI ARABIA
$0.5T 0.72%

WORLD REGION
- Australia
- Rest of the World
- Latin America and Caribbean
- Middle East
- Europe
- Asia
- North America

T = trillion

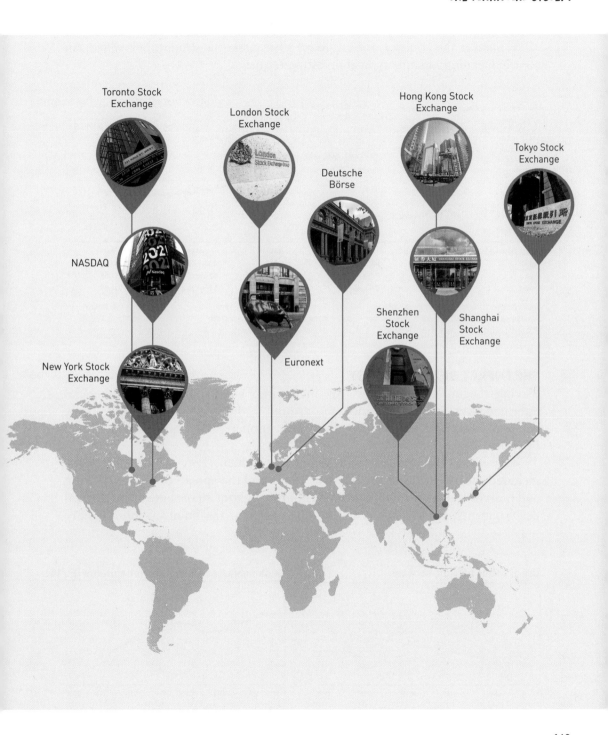

Toronto Stock Exchange

London Stock Exchange

Hong Kong Stock Exchange

Tokyo Stock Exchange

Deutsche Börse

NASDAQ

Shenzhen Stock Exchange

Shanghai Stock Exchange

New York Stock Exchange

Euronext

Whatever the country, the language of investing is similar. Below we can see the meaning of some typical investing terms:

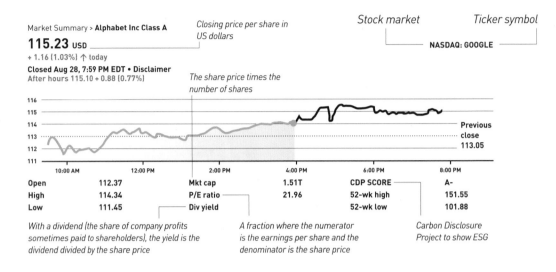

THE IMPACT OF TECHNOLOGY

Having begun this chapter by imagining how, pumped by financial intermediaries, money moves around the circular flow, now we can consider how the flow of money has been transformed by technology.

The results are evident and somewhat hidden. Previous changes have included the invention of the ATM in 1967, and the spread of online banking and online retail in more recent times. But throughout all of these technological developments, banks have remained the center of the financial intermediary universe.

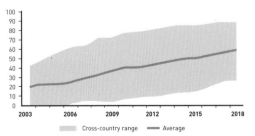

Use of online banking services

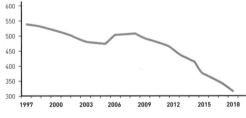

Bank branches per million inhabitants (EU15)

Focusing on the EU, we see computer use way up and bank employee numbers down. Access to low-cost digital data enhances the quantity and quality of information on which banks base their loan-making decisions. The data includes applicants' non-financial details, which allows the banks to make "better" predictions about a loanee's likelihood of defaulting on their repayments. As banking activity moves more and more online, branches become less important and banks become less local.

Charles Dow (left) and Edward Jones (right).

Technology also facilitates the flow of information. In 1883, the New York-based business journalists Charles Dow and Edward Jones began writing a daily financial newsletter containing information investors might want to know. It was delivered around the city to interested parties by messenger, and to more distant locations by carrier pigeon (occasionally). Today, phones and computers allow information to be shared instantly, and for truly tech-savvy traders there are large profits to be found in the fractions of a second between a stock's price rising or falling and whether they (or, increasingly, an automated app) decide to buy or sell it.

At the same time, to check market activity or the price of a security, you and I might keep an eye on the Tokyo Stock Exchange through the Nikkei Index, or the FTSE (Financial Times Stock Exchange, pronounced "Footsie"), an index of 100 companies listed on the London Stock Exchange. For the US, we might go to the S&P (Standard and Poor's) 500. Depending on the information we need, we would have a long list of the world's stock indexes from which to choose. All have immediately accessible information on which we can base our investing decisions.

Digital Currencies

As the pre-eminent digital currency, Bitcoin represents the attempt to entirely sidestep the regulatory constraints of traditional banking and securities. Called a digital currency or cryptocurrency (though regulators debate whether it is a security rather than a commodity), Bitcoin opens the door to a slew of other exclusively digital forms of payment, yet it is not universally accepted. Unconstrained by traditional central bankers, digital currencies are in a different world—they have a fixed amount of currency in existence, and for most digital currencies, more can only be created through a resource-intensive process known as "mining," which uses high-powered computers to solve complex mathematical problems. There is no central authority that can create or remove Bitcoins, which makes it tough for central banks to control money supply and interest rates. So too do the "shadow banks" that are not necessarily banks but provide loans through the securities they sell. Bitcoin and shadow banks are just two examples of non-bank entities providing services that had always been the exclusive preserve of the banks. They take us to a new "marketplace" in which banks have to compete not just with each other but against entities and institutions that are not like them at all. It is an arena in which regulatory authorities, consumers, and businesses and municipalities must adjust their behavior. They avoid the explicit impact of financial intermediaries on economic policy.

ECONOMIC POLICY
Financial intermediaries play a crucial role pumping money and credit around the circular flow of a market economy. By looking at four "linking graphs" (see opposite) we can see how they connect to the monetary and fiscal policies that deal with inflation, recession, and unemployment.

Taking inflation as our example, let's assume that policymakers have to deal with inflation that exceeds a 2 percent annual target. Because controlling inflation was our goal, we started the chain reaction in Step 1 with tight money policy from the central bank. By the time we reached our AD/AS graph, we constrained the price level. However, if unemployment and a contracting economy were the problem, then you would move the money supply to the right in the linking graph. The monetary sequence would then move in the opposite direction. At the "end," the price level would rise, as would output.

Whichever direction the ripple moves, at this point we can include stock and bond markets. When loanable funds become cheaper, investors have the incentive to borrow more of them. Correspondingly, higher interest rates constrain the investors that borrow. Both affect the markets that determine securities' prices and the individuals, businesses, and governments that want to buy and sell them.

1

We can start with the money supply graph that the Federal Reserve directly manipulates. The vertical line is the US money supply while the downward sloping line represents the demand for money. Below, the arrow points to the left because the goal is to contract the money supply and elevate interest rates. We typically want to contract the money supply and/or elevate interest rates when the value of money is decreasing because of an excessively high inflation rate:

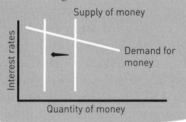

2

From here, we can see the Federal Reserve affecting the supply of loanable funds in banks. By diminishing the quantity of money, they reduce the supply of loanable funds. Again we see higher interest rates:

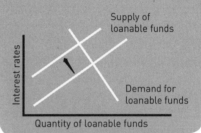

4

From here we can go to what economists call aggregate demand and supply because they represent the entire economy. Whereas most aggregate demand comes from GDP components—consumption, gross investment, and government spending, aggregate supply relates to the land, labor, and capital in the US economy. On our AD/AS graph, when the GDP investment component became less active, then so too did economic activity. On the graph, real GDP declines as does the price level:

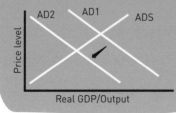

3

Our next step is an investment graph. Representing the GDP definition of investment, we are looking at business spending on new construction, new tools and equipment, on research and development, on inventories, and consumers spending for new homes. As a downward sloping curve, we have an inverse relationship between interest rates and investment. When loanable funds went down, interest rates went up. Consequently, on an investment graph, investment activity also diminishes:

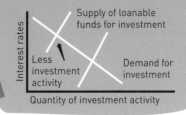

Economic Growth

Returning to where we began, we can remember that in the securities markets through which fortunes are made and lost, we invest in countless different ways. And, as we save and (hopefully) grow our wealth, securities markets connect us to the investors that can productively use our money and fuel economic growth.

The graph below not only illustrates the shifting composition of stock market activity but, most crucially, shows a blueprint for economic growth. Those transports in blue were the railroads that connected regions and let them specialize. Through stocks and bonds, railroads got the money that let them lay track, move goods, and transport people. The utilities included electrification. When it was possible to have lighting 24 hours a day, seven days a week, it meant that we did not have to shut down most forms of economic activity in the hours of darkness. The "productive" day expanded from roughly eight hours to 24 hours. At the same time, markets from the late 19th century funded the steel and coal and capital goods industries that formed a foundation for further economic development. The 20th century saw the further growth of industry accompanied by the massive expansion of the consumer goods sector, with its automobiles, TVs, radios, and washing machines. Leaping forward to the present day, we have the tech and information industries.

As a whole, we can see that financial intermediaries were crucial for sending savers' money to the investing firms and governments that grew a country's economy. Securities markets can catapult developing nations from low income countries to more affluent ones by funding their new businesses.

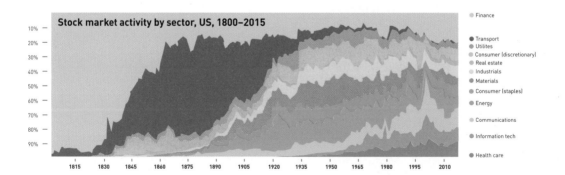

Stock market activity by sector, US, 1800–2015

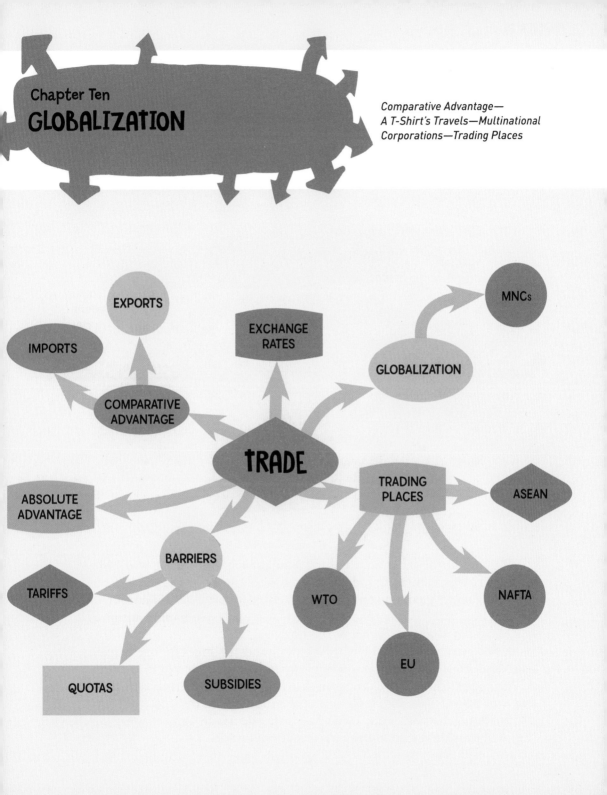

GLOBALIZATION

Comparative Advantage—
A T-Shirt's Travels—Multinational
Corporations—Trading Places

MNCs

EXPORTS

EXCHANGE
RATES

GLOBALIZATION

IMPORTS

COMPARATIVE
ADVANTAGE

TRADE

TRADING
PLACES

ASEAN

ABSOLUTE
ADVANTAGE

BARRIERS

WTO

NAFTA

TARIFFS

EU

QUOTAS

SUBSIDIES

A circular flow model can have a reach far beyond national borders when large and small corporations send goods and services to distant markets. Arriving abroad, those goods and services are subject to the local laws and international institutions that establish the rules of trade. Connecting people, businesses, and governments, globalization can create the incentives that boost productivity, encourage innovation, and support growth.

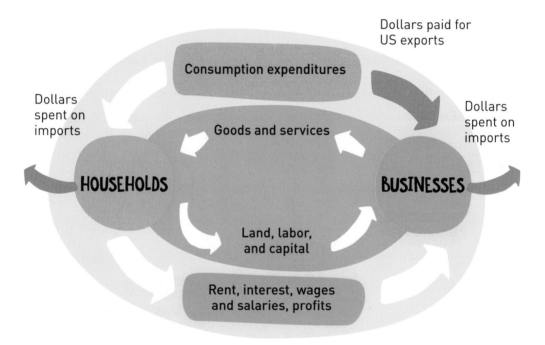

Looking at the label on a t-shirt, it might tell you that it was "Made in China." Labels, it turns out, don't tell the whole story. However, it is possible that a factory in Vietnam spun the yarn from raw cotton that it imported from India. Then, after China made the shirt, it could have wound up in one of H&M's many stores in the US or the UK.

Asked why a t-shirt might travel thousands of miles before reaching its final destination, an economist would say two words: comparative advantage. And it is the concept of comparative advantage and the travels of a t-shirt that will provide our first look at globalization. From there, we will consider multinational corporations, trade barriers, and trade agreements. Together, they will provide our snapshot of international trade.

COMPARATIVE ADVANTAGE

Counterintuitively, the best place to make a t-shirt is not necessarily where people are best at making it. Instead, we have to consider absolute advantage and comparative advantage. A country has the absolute advantage for a task when it does it better than anyone else, anywhere else. Somewhat differently, you have the comparative advantage when doing something requires less of a sacrifice. An economist would say that having a comparative advantage means your opportunity cost is less. Comparative advantage determines where items should be made.

Thinking of people, we can say that, when she was at the height of her abilities, Serena Williams had the absolute advantage for playing tennis because she was the best. But what if she was also the best at mowing her lawn? Should she do both? That would mean that when she mowed her lawn, she could not play tennis.

At this point we need a neighbor to complete the story. Assume that this neighbor—who offers to mow her lawn—has a part-time job at McDonald's that pays $15 an hour. If Serena mows the lawn, her opportunity cost is more hours of practicing and playing tennis. By contrast, her neighbor sacrifices the $15 he would have earned at McDonald's. Seeing these numbers, an economist would say that the neighbor should mow Serena's lawn as long as she pays him more than $15 and less than she earns, because Serena has the comparative advantage for tennis while her neighbor has the comparative advantage for mowing lawns.

Serena Williams		
Alternatives	**Tennis**	**Mowing the Lawn**
Benefits	Practice time + Money earned	Save $20
Decision	Practice tennis	
Opportunity Cost		Sacrifice the lawn
The Neighbor		
Alternatives	**McDonald's**	**Mowing the Lawn**
Benefits	$15	Earns $20
Decision		Mow the lawn
Opportunity Cost	Sacrifice McDonald's	

Because Serena and the neighbor sacrifice the least, they each have the comparative advantage for what they wind up doing.

And, according to the principle of comparative advantage, both gain from the trade. He has more money and she has more practice time. The key is what they would have sacrificed. Comparing the lawn to tennis practice, the tennis would have been the bigger loss for Serena. But the neighbor only had McDonald's to sacrifice when he mowed Serena's lawn.

> **ABSOLUTE ADVANTAGE** ▶ *an economic principle that indicates one producer (i.e. a nation) can make a good or service with fewer inputs than another producer.*

> **COMPARATIVE ADVANTAGE** ▶ *an economic principle that suggests the world will get the highest gains from trade when each nation produces the goods and services for which it has the lowest opportunity cost.*

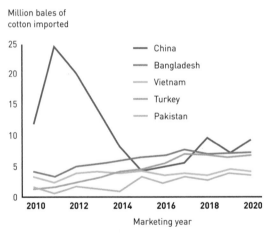

We can hypothesize that the world's leading cotton importers have a comparative advantage for making t-shirts.

T-Shirts and Comparative Advantage

For the same reason that Serena Williams should play tennis and not mow her lawn, t-shirt production is shared by different nations. Whether it's tennis or a t-shirt, through comparative advantage, everyone optimizes production by minimizing their opportunity cost. If, for example, the US or UK were to make t-shirts with their land, labor, and capital, a more productive alternative would be sacrificed.

Next, making the decision even more logical, in Chapter 5 we saw how Malcom McLean made shipping cost several pennies rather than many dollars by developing the container ship. Correspondingly, the numbers become huge when one ship carries 24,000 containers, each with space for 80,000 t-shirts. Indeed, looking at a history of globalization, we became more interconnected when technology shrunk the world. It related to the railroads that grew a transportation infrastructure, and to the communications infrastructure that spread information through telegraph, telephone, undersea cables, and computers. Adding to the synergy, we have a financial infrastructure that enabled an international network of banks and securities markets to connect buyers and sellers in distant places. Considering the results, an economist would say the world benefits from the growth that comparative advantage optimizes.

1500–1840
Average speed of horse-drawn coaches and sailing ships: 10 mph (16 km/h)

1850–1930
Average speed of steam locomotives: 65 mph (105 km/h)
Average speed of steam ships: 36 mph (58 km/h)

1950s
Average speed of propeller aircraft:
300–400 mph (483–644 km/h)

1960s
Average speed of jet passenger aircraft:
500–700 mph (805–1126 km/h)

Transport innovation shrunk the world.

A T-SHIRT'S TRAVELS

But let's take a closer look.

The t-shirt we will accompany was purchased from Walgreens by an economics professor, Pietra Rivoli, who described its journey in *The Travels of a T-Shirt in the Global Economy* (2009). Including many people and places, her book might instead have been called *A Tale of Comparative Advantage*.

Our t-shirt started its journey near Lubbock, Texas, on the Reinsch Farm. Located at the convergence of university and government support, Lubbock's cotton farmers have benefited from university research and financial subsidies from the government. They've planted genetically modified seeds, used increasingly better fertilizer, and enjoyed the massive productivity that only capital can create. As a result, the six million bales of cotton that Texas produced in 2020 could have become a mind-boggling 7.2 billion t-shirts.

We need only look at the John Deere 7760 cotton stripper to see why such massive productivity is possible. Priced in the vicinity of $600,000, it is a self-driving robot that, with one driver, takes in the cotton at the front and spits out bales at the back. Eliminating the need for 10 or 11 farm employees, the John Deere 7760, and devices like it, made it possible for 13 people and 26 machines to produce annually 13,000 bales of cotton that could become millions of t-shirts.

China

Leaving Texas for China, the Reinsch farm's cotton entered a grading system that identified all a buyer needed to know about fiber color, length, and strength. From there, in China, the raw cotton became yarn, fabric, and, finally, a t-shirt.

For the shirt that we are following, the Reinsch cotton probably headed west from Texas to a Pacific Coast port. We should note that, in 2022, it was just as likely that the raw cotton would have gone to Bangladesh, Vietnam, Indonesia, Mexico, Thailand, South Korea, or Pakistan as China.

In China, the first stop was the Shanghai Number 36 Cotton Yarn Factory. To make yarn, the bales had to be cleaned by vacuum-like devices. Next, the cotton was blown apart and then flattened until it could be pulled into a "snowy rope." Out of that sequence, we got strands of thread that became spools.

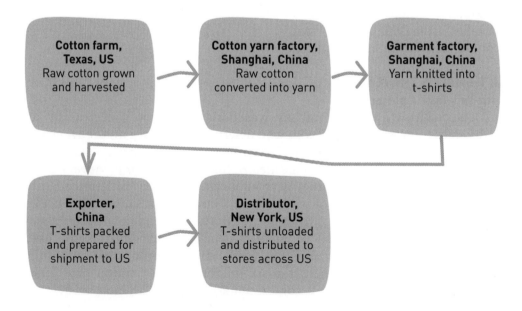

The yarn's last home in China was the Shanghai Brightness Number 3 Garment Factory's knitting machines. An economist might say we have moved from a mechanized stage of production to a labor-intensive stage (the cotton harvesting, using the John Deere 7760, and the yarn-making operation all use more machinery than people in the production process, whereas sewing requires one person to use each sewing machine). Each person at each sewing machine works on different parts of the t-shirt, completing the sleeves, collar, and hem.

Finally ready to leave China, the t-shirt travels to an exporter, Shanghai Knitwear. They do the logistical planning for the trip to Florida, where a US silk-screening firm will prepare it for Walgreens. Carrying container boxes, each loaded with as many as 80,000 t-shirts, the ship leaves China, passes through the Panama Canal, and docks at a US East Coast port. On arrival, the container shifts from the boat to a train or truck and unloads the contents for silk-screening. After its sale at Walgreens and some time with a buyer, the t-shirt could be donated to the Salvation Army. From there, it enters a world market in secondhand clothing. At this point our t-shirt again becomes an export, destined perhaps for Malaysia or Pakistan or India.

A container ship passes through the Panama Canal.

MULTINATIONAL CORPORATIONS

Our t-shirt and countless other goods are world travelers because of the corporations that facilitate their journeys. Long ago, businesses expanded beyond their home borders. As Adam Smith explained, trade enabled economies of scale when bigger markets complemented ever-expanding mass production.

But while it's clear that economic phenomena are never that simple, we can generalize with a company that starts in one place and then exports its goods elsewhere. Eventually, it could decide to open a foreign factory and thereby establish a foreign direct investment. At that point, having become multinational, companies start to take on the identity and culture of the place where they have located a subsidiary.

It all began in the United States when Isaac Singer patented his version of the sewing machine in 1851. Revolutionizing garment manufacture, the sewing machine was sold in 14 different markets in the US. From there, the company got foreign patents, sold selling rights to foreign representatives, and opened far-off company-owned stores in places such as Peru, Germany, Scotland, and Russia.

As demand for Singer sewing machines grew in Russia in particular, the company had to decide whether to oversee distant sales from New York, to run the Russian venture from Germany, or to establish a separate Russian subsidiary. Ultimately, Singer chose the latter option, in part because it allowed them to sidestep German taxes and Russian tariffs. A factory was established close to Moscow, and soon its 1,000 employees had built up an inventory of 68,000 machines. It was only with the outbreak of the Russian Revolution in 1917 that things began to change. Once the Bolsheviks took power, Singer—like the Osorgins—had to go.

The global spread of Coca-Cola is slightly different from Singer. Established in 1886, Coca-Cola first emerged as a fountain drink in an Atlanta, Georgia, drug store. By manufacturing and selling its syrup while others did most of the bottling, the company grew quickly. Within 40 years, Coke had become a national drink.

When Coca-Cola decided to expand beyond the US, it sold its syrup to local bottlers or opened its own bottling plants. This did not go so well in France, at least initially, where the bottles were not properly sanitized. A number of customers complained of suffering from nausea (and worse, although reputedly no one died).

Coca-Cola discovered that each country was unique. In London, it was decided (for tax purposes) to export the syrup through a Canadian subsidiary, since Canada was a member of the Commonwealth. Controlled by Coca-Cola, a British corporation ran the bottling initiative. In Indonesia, Coca-Cola had to create the infrastructure. It had to build glass manufacturers and bottling plants. Transport was a consideration. By contrast, their German operation, with too many bottlers, needed consolidation. Everywhere, the challenge was a balancing act between local tastes and global standardization.

The Singer sewing machine of 1851.

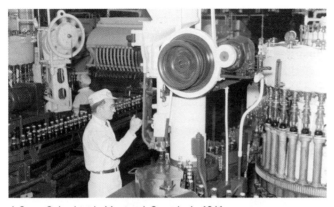

A Coca-Cola plant in Montreal, Canada, in 1941.

So, whether it is 1920 or 2020, and we are talking about sewing machines, t-shirts, or Coca-Cola factories, the stories for each are both similar and timeless. The protagonists are the corporations that began locally, extended beyond their national borders with exports, and then hired foreign representatives. Some established the factories that let them call a distant nation their new home and others had supply chains along which they gathered components.

The one constant was the multinational corporation that had a strategy and structure through which it made and sold goods and services in different nations. The result was the lengthy supply chains that enabled items like our t-shirt to travel 40,000 miles (64,370 km) during which, raised by a multinational parent, it gradually became a finished global product.

TRADING PLACES

As economists, though, we should ask what determines whether a country is an importer or an exporter. One answer is the market. When, because of supply and demand, the domestic prices of commodities and manufactured goods are higher than elsewhere, those cheaper foreign goods become imports. Correspondingly, if they are more expensive abroad, then producers have the incentive to export their items and sell them in world markets.

IMPORTS ▶ *the goods and services that are produced outside of a nation and then sent and (potentially) sold inside that country.*

EXPORTS ▶ *the goods and services that are produced domestically, and then sent and (potentially) sold outside that country.*

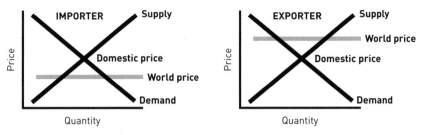

The world price can determine if a country is an exporter or an importer.

Depending on where we look, we would frequently see that trade occupies a significant proportion of many nations' GDP. More recently, however, *The Economist* tells us that, from 2008 to 2019, the size of world trade in relation to global GDP has shrunk. One reason is trade barriers.

TRADE-TO-GDP RATIO, BY COUNTRY

| No data | 0% | 20% | 50% | 100% | 200% | 500% |

Each nation's trade-to-GDP ratio lets us identify the world's trading nations.

Trade Barriers

The problems (or benefits, depending on your perspective) start when one country wants to protect its domestic producers with tariffs, quotas, and/or subsidies. As a tax on imports, tariffs elevate the prices of goods that enter the country. Somewhat similarly, reducing the number of imports through a quota can also eliminate domestic price pressure. A third approach is the subsidy. The money received from a subsidy can create a price floor when a firm's income shrinks or enable that firm to charge less, lower the world price, and compete unfairly. Again, vastly simplifying, whether the barrier is a tariff, a quota, or a subsidy, the result is less price and quality competition, and more room in the market for domestic jobs and production.

TARIFF ▶ *a tax on imports.*

QUOTAS ▶ *limited quantities of imports established by a government.*

SUBSIDIES ▶ *when given by a government, the money directly or indirectly received by a producer of a good or a service to offset an insufficient market price.*

WORLD PRICE ▶ *the equilibrium price determined by supply and demand in world markets for goods and services.*

Exchange Rates

Less obvious as trade barriers or trade facilitators, the price of a currency can boost trade or reduce it. Just like everyday goods and services, supply and demand can determine if money is more or less valuable. Looked at simply, we can say that currencies become stronger or weaker. They can appreciate in value or depreciate. Because a stronger appreciated currency is more expensive, it makes the goods and services exported by the nation using that currency less attractive. Correspondingly, a weaker, depreciated currency can make exports more desirable.

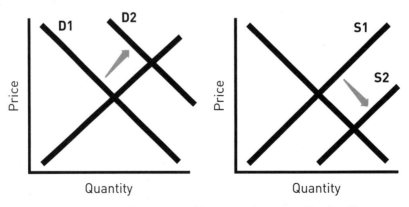

When investors increase the demand for currency #1, they need currency #2 to "buy" it.

Shown by graphs, we can start with currency #1 and assume that higher interest rates made its country's bonds more attractive to foreign investors. Needing money to buy those bonds, investors increase the global demand for currency #1. Correspondingly, they need more of their own currency to buy that money, thereby raising its supply. Using classic supply and demand, we see currency #1 goes up in price and the other currency goes down.

And yes, it all connects to our t-shirt. The value of a currency can make a t-shirt more or less expensive. It affects the prices of a vast menu of imports and exports.

Trade Agreements
Like more traditional conflicts, nations have negotiated international trade agreements to minimize trade wars. The goal was free trade. The result was a cascade of letters and acronyms. Here are a few.

EU
The story of the European Union began more than 70 years ago with a limited economic partnership between France and what was then West Germany. However, by 1951, the Netherlands, Luxembourg, Belgium, and Italy had joined them to form a six-nation free trade zone for coal and steel. With goods, services, consumers, and workers moving ever more effortlessly across European borders, that free trade zone grew, and the rest is history.

USMCA
Recently renegotiated among the US, Canada, and Mexico, and renamed USMCA (United States-Mexico-Canada Agreement), NAFTA (as it had traditionally been called, standing for North American Free Trade Agreement) created the fruits of free trade and so much more. Because of NAFTA, the US has an abundance of strawberries, avocados, cantaloupes, and limes. It has unfinished cars effortlessly moving from Mexico to the US and then back again as they are gradually assembled.

WTO
Composed of 164 nations, the World Trade Organization has articulated the rules for free trade and the institutions that enforce and interpret them. When Brazil, for example, felt that US cotton subsidies were unfair, it took its complaint to the WTO. The WTO decision compelled the US to either eliminate the subsidies or help Brazilian farmers. It chose to send cash payments to Brazilian cotton farmers for a limited amount of time.

Regional and Bilateral Agreements

Even with the number of regional trade agreements increasing from 50 in 1990 to more than 250 in 2022, new deals are still being negotiated. One example is the African Continental Free Trade Area agreement, AfCFTA. According to the World Bank, AfCFTA could make a substantial difference for its 55 signatories. By minimizing tariff and non-tariff trade barriers, and harmonizing e-commerce, intellectual property, and investment policies, the agreement is supposed to help smaller businesses become part of a larger supply chain. By replacing the region's commodity dependence with diversification, incomes are expected to rise and extreme poverty decrease.

Indeed, whether in Africa, Asia, or beyond, the goal of freer trade remains the regional consistency that facilitates foreign investment and one market. It is supposed to align national policies and eliminate bureaucratic procedures. The goal of free trade is less friction. Whether it's two nations or 20, regional trade agreements diminish the friction that slows or prevents transactions. They align national policies and eliminate bureaucratic procedures. They facilitate the benefits of comparative advantage.

Free trade areas

United States

United Kingdom, overseas territories, and dependencies

Agreement in current effect

Agreement being negotiated

Displaying new trade patterns, these maps show some of the bilateral agreements observed by the US and the UK.

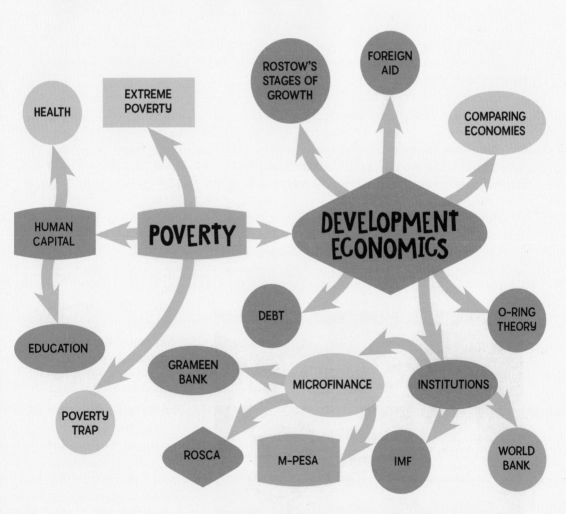

Chapter Eleven
DEVELOPMENT ECONOMICS

*Two Sisters—Development
Definitions—Development Strategies—
Poverty—Human Capital—Debt*

HEALTH

EXTREME POVERTY

ROSTOW'S STAGES OF GROWTH

FOREIGN AID

COMPARING ECONOMIES

HUMAN CAPITAL

POVERTY

DEVELOPMENT ECONOMICS

EDUCATION

DEBT

O-RING THEORY

POVERTY TRAP

GRAMEEN BANK

MICROFINANCE

INSTITUTIONS

ROSCA

M-PESA

IMF

WORLD BANK

Next we turn to look at the parts of the world, containing nearly 7 billion people, where living standards are lower. As elsewhere, scarcity remains the key economic problem and we need to ask the same three economic questions. We still calculate GDP and consider income. However, we need also to ask about poverty, health, education, and finance.

TWO SISTERS

Our story begins with two sisters. Prabhati and Shashi Das were born and raised in a traditional village in northeast India. Then, one day in 2016, they left. Initially, this was because their family was poor and could not afford dowries for them if they were to marry. Having left the family home, the sisters decided to stay away, opting for the freedom offered by working in a garment factory over the security of the village life.

Had they stayed at home, their destinies would have been very different. Their parents would have selected husbands for them, and chaperones would have accompanied them on the few, if any, "dates" they would have gone on with their future partners. Once married, they would have left their own household and moved in with their husband and his family—where they would have demonstrated their submission by washing the feet of their new in-laws each morning.

But they did not stay home. Instead, their father accepted a payment equivalent to around $6.75 for each of his daughters from a "mobilizer"—a person contracted by the Indian government to recruit workers. Soon, Prabhati and Shashi, aged 21 and 19 respectively, were taking their first-ever train journey, heading hundreds of miles south to the city of Bangalore.

After two months of training, the girls were earning more than the typical income of a household in their home village. In exchange, they might have had to sew 100 tags an hour onto shirts for eight hours a day, with a half-hour break for lunch. The pay was around $2 a day, with Sundays off.

A traditional house in an Indian village.

They lived and slept with the other factory workers. While their days were tedious and exhausting, for the first time they earned their own money and could choose a boyfriend, buy a phone, and enjoy the free time they had doing whatever they wished. The "cost" of their new world was the tradition, security, and predictability of what they had left behind.

These two young women take us firsthand to understanding the idea of development. As we look at poverty, human capital, and debt, they remind us that what we are really talking about is people.

DEVELOPMENT DEFINITIONS

Scholars have defined development as more than the process through which economies move from low to high income. It also encompasses overcoming the problems of poverty, of empowering women, and of rural-to-urban migration, amongst other things. The Indian economist, philosopher, and Nobel laureate Amartya Sen equated development with freedom. Through poor health, a lack of education, a low quality of life, and the inability to achieve your ambitions, poverty shackles people's ability to aspire to higher goals. Ill health, for example, can limit our freedom of choice, as will lack of empowerment within the family. The common theme among the long list of development definitions is the human cost that must be borne.

People experiencing the most extreme poverty consume food lacking the basic nutrients, they live in homes with insufficient sanitation, space, and heat, and their drinking water is probably contaminated. People and households on the income ladder that have slightly more may live in rural or urban areas, have access to water through a tap, and own a basic means of transport such as a used bicycle. On the next rung of our ladder of affluence, we see families with televisions, motorbikes or mopeds, and children with lower infant mortality rates. Jobs tend to be informal and not very stable compared to those higher up the ladder.

Overcoming poverty

Empowering women

Health and education

Aspects of development

Economic growth

Rural to urban migration

Income

Through per capita GNI (gross national income), the World Bank's analysis allows us to compare 217 economies. Moving from the lowest per capita incomes to the higher bands, we can see the four layers that make up the world's earnings. We can identify low-income countries (LICs), lower-middle-income countries (LMCs), upper-middle-income countries (UMCs), and high-income countries (HICs). Although there are some exceptions, by looking at the LICs, LMCs, and UMCs we can see which are the world's developing nations.

Group	Per capita income range (July 1, 2021)	Economy examples
Low-income	<$1,085	**Total number of economies:** 28 **Examples:** Burundi, Chad, Ethiopia
Lower-middle-income	$1,086–$4,255	**Total number of economies:** 54 **Examples:** Haiti, Indonesia
Upper-middle-income	$4,256–$13,205	**Total number of economies:** 54 **Examples:** Moldova, Panama, Romania
High-income	>$13,2055	**Total number of economies:** 81 **Examples:** US, Japan, Australia

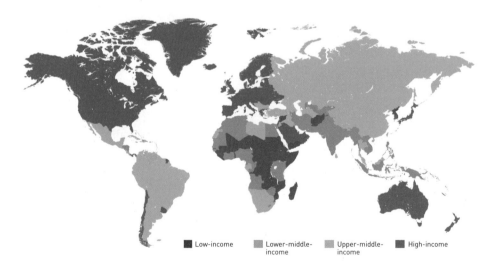

Low-income Lower-middle-income Upper-middle-income High-income

The greens and purples differentiate the high- and low-income countries.

DEVELOPMENT STRATEGIES

The task of development is to elevate people's lives and capabilities. How to do this has been debated for many decades. In their earliest theories, economists described a linear theory of development. One of the most famous was the theory popularized by Walt W. Rostow that showed five stages of development taking place in order. In a 1959 paper, he said the sequence began with a traditional society, continued with the preconditions for "takeoff," and then unfolded through the takeoff, the "drive to maturity," and the "age of high mass consumption." Most crucially, self-sustaining growth came after the takeoff point. When countries followed the rules and generated sufficient domestic and foreign savings, they could make it to high income.

But there are other pathways to development.

Rather than a linear sequence, other strategies focus on the structures that could make an agriculturally-anchored economy more diverse, for example. Then, characterized by dependence and dominance, yet another approach looks at past colonial status as the key to moving forward. These international dependence models emphasize the constraints created through relationships with richer countries. And, of course, we cannot forget the market advocates who say that supply and demand best allocate the resources that developing economies need.

Indeed, we could have devoted an entire book to each development approach. But our key here is to emphasize that development economics has a varied toolkit that targets incomes and human intangibles.

DEVELOPMENT ECONOMICS ▶ *the study of how the incomes, the human capital, and the power of people in lower-income countries can increase.*

POVERTY

Knowing that development requires elevating GNI, we need to ask who will make it grow. That takes us to poverty, and focusing on the people with living standards that need to rise.

Our first step is a definition of poverty. In 2022, the World Bank moved the poverty line up to those living on $2.15 or less a day. When the extreme (or absolute) poverty line was at $1.90 in 2017, close to 750 million people lived beneath it. At this point, you might be thinking that it is impossible to have one poverty line for everybody. And yes, that would be correct. In Ethiopia, $2.15 can purchase far more than it could in the United States. So we can see different poverty lines for different countries—it is more realistic to cite $2.04 per day in Ethiopia and $24.55 in the United States, based on 2017 figures.

Recognizing disparities, economists have asked how to compare income statistics from different countries. The answer is the common currency that they can create using purchasing power parity (PPP). PPP lets us compare the prices of the same basket of goods and services in different countries. We ask, for example, how much of Country X's currency we need to buy the same basket of goods in Country X and also in Country Y. The difference lets us create a common currency that organizations such as the World Bank can use to compare statistics like poverty levels or GDPs. The World Bank tells us that the PPP of South Africa to the US would be 4.77 if 363 South African Rand (ZAR) are what a US 50 dollar basket of goods and services should cost with an exchange rate of 7.26. However, since the cost in South Africa is actually 239 ZAR, we divide 239 by 50 to get the PPP of 4.77.

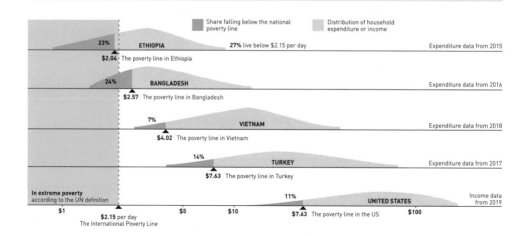

PURCHASING POWER PARITY (PPP) ▶ *a method of creating a common currency by comparing the prices of the same basket of goods in different countries. World organizations use PPPs to calculate comparable statistics like poverty levels and GDPs.*

Share falling below the national poverty line

Distribution of household expenditure or income

ETHIOPIA 23% — 27% live below $2.15 per day — Expenditure data from 2015
$2.04 The poverty line in Ethiopia

BANGLADESH 24% — Expenditure data from 2016
$2.57 The poverty line in Bangladesh

VIETNAM 7% — Expenditure data from 2018
$4.02 The poverty line in Vietnam

TURKEY 14% — Expenditure data from 2017
$7.63 The poverty line in Turkey

In extreme poverty according to the UN definition

UNITED STATES 11% — Income data from 2019

$1 $5 $10 $100
$2.15 per day
The International Poverty Line
$7.63 The poverty line in the US

The households with the highest childhood mortality rates, the shortest lives, and the least education live close to the poverty line in the world's low-income countries. In a low-income country, the mortality rate for children under five could be 12.7 percent, while a young girl might attend school for less than five years.

That said, we do have less extreme poverty than 200 years ago, when three quarters of the people in the world lived without the basics. In 2017, because of economic growth, the extreme poverty share of the world's population was close to 10 percent.

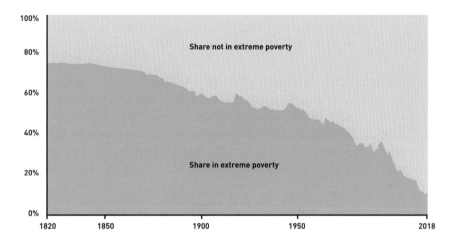

The global extreme poverty line includes approximately 10 percent of the world's population.

EXTREME POVERTY ▶ *defined as living beneath the World Bank's income threshold of $2.15 a day, but also including intangibles such as lack of prestige and power.*

Eliminating Extreme Poverty

There is more to eliminating extreme poverty than increasing national income. Among the causes of poverty, development economists cite low human capital (see page 193) and political and social exclusion. Consequently, they point out that as incomes rise, prestige, power, and gender imbalance need also to shift. In addition, they ask how to help "the many" when GNI grows instead of the few with influence or money.

In her book Poor Economics, *Nobel laureate Esther Duflo uses an S-shape curve to illustrate the poverty trap. The poverty trap moves individuals earning a wage of A1 to the lower income, A3, along the left end of the x-axis.*

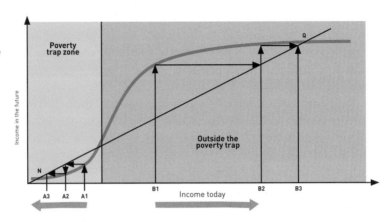

One problem is a poverty trap through which hardship is perpetuated for a family or a nation in a vicious cycle in which poverty begets more poverty. Identifying the causes of that poverty is one thing; devising ways of escape for those affected by it is another. We might need to investigate the fertilizer market if that is one farmer's problem. It might involve the unavailability of credit or a lack of savings for someone else, or inadequate nutrition for yet another person.

At this point, economists do not necessarily agree on the best method of breaking out of a poverty trap's vicious cycle. One group, for example, has suggested that foreign investment helps to diminish extreme poverty; others think that any lift, to be long-lasting, has to come from within the household. Michael Kremer, who received the 2019 Nobel Memorial Prize in Economic Sciences with Esther Duflo and Abhijit Banerjee, has expressed an "O-ring" theory of economic development. Named after the cause of the 1986 *Challenger* space shuttle disaster, when a flawed O-ring

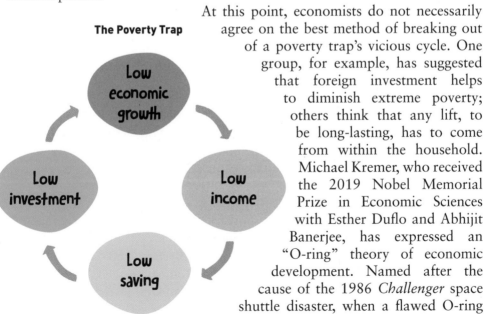

The Poverty Trap

seal initiated a series of failures, Kremer's ideas suggest that in firms and countries, lower-skilled individuals interact to perpetuate their own poverty. Like the O-ring, among the poor, we can have one problem that cascades to create others. By contrast, interactions among higher-skilled individuals create the incentive to become more skilled.

The requisites for shedding poverty in the home and at work depend on more than one variable. At home, health needs to meet a minimum. In the factory, all workers need to improve their skills. In each instance, failure of one factor pulls the other down and reinforces the poverty trap. Consequently, Dr. Duflo tells us that development economists need to collect the right data to accurately grasp what is happening.

POVERTY TRAP ▶ *where a network of variables prevent individuals from diminishing poverty.*

When Esther Duflo won the 2019 Nobel Memorial Prize in Economic Sciences with her husband Abhijit Banerjee and Michael Kremer, it was a recognition of their pioneering work with field experiments. By directing their economic lens from the bottom up rather than the top down, Dr. Duflo and her colleagues answered specific questions about poverty that could be used for bigger policy decisions.

They investigated, for example, why a $400 billion new stove project in India flopped. Its goal was to empower women and improve health by replacing traditional open-fire stoves with closed ovens that polluted less. By talking to the stove users, they discovered that the new stoves were not popular because they were attached to chimneys and therefore could not be moved outside, they broke down easily, and they cooked food more slowly than their old stoves. Consequently, four years after the new stoves had been introduced, most of them had been abandoned by their users.

Explaining their approach, Dr. Banerjee said that the "hyper-rational being that lives in economic models" did not know how real people would react in many real-world situations. Seeking to break away from those models, Banerjee, Duflo, and Kremer adopted instead a more human-focused approach. When looking at particular issues—such as the take-up rate for new stoves, or whether to charge for mosquito nets or give them away—the trio of economists set up control groups similar to those used in pharmaceutical trials. This allowed them to see how individuals and groups exposed to or withheld from specific situations would actually react. One important outcome of the work undertaken by Duflo, Banerjee, and Kremer is to remind us that alleviating poverty is about more than elevating incomes; it is about understanding the lives of those who live in poverty, too.

In a similar way, Michael Kremer used a "nudge" approach to solve a chlorination problem. When pipes deliver water to homes in the US or the UK, for example, it has already been purified and chlorinated, so that the water is ready and safe to drink. But for those living in poorer developing nations and whose water comes from a well, they have to remember to add chlorine drops to the water when they take it home. Kremer's suggestion was to add a "one turn" chlorine dispenser next to the well that was free to use and easy to operate, and which introduced the correct amount of chlorine into a person's water container. After "one-turn" dispensers were installed next to wells they served as a more immediate reminder to users of the need to chlorinate their water. Following their introduction, randomized trials showed there were fewer instances of diarrhea in communities whose wells had "one-turn" dispensers close by.

In another nudge experiment, Esther Duflo tried to harness the power of a default in regard to fortified flour. In Duflo's program, villagers were told they could have their flour automatically fortified with anemia-preventing iron if they selected the default option. This, in retrospect, may have been a mistake as people had to actively opt in to the program (whereas presenting participants with an opt-out option is usually more effective). In addition, the default option for the millers involved in the experiment was to not add iron to the flour unless they were asked—meaning that they too had to opt in to the program.

A traditional Indian open-fired stove.

This double opt-in scenario probably explains why Duflo's experiment did not work. As she explained in her book *Poor Economics*, "the small cost of having to insist on fortification was large enough to discourage most people." But in the program's failure lies a clue as to how to make nudges more efficient and maximize the possibilities of implementing defaults: the reduction of friction. In short, where possible arrange default programs so that participants must opt out rather than opt in.

HUMAN CAPITAL

The development focus on poverty takes economists to human capital (the skills and knowledge of the population). Necessary for boosting our capabilities and productivity, the health and education components of human capital are essential for technological progress. Looking at health as a prerequisite for education and then at how the two elevate income, we can see how, interwoven, the three march upward together.

Health

Nobel laureate Richard Fogel has suggested that we can use height to judge health. His evidence relates to the increase in average height during the past two centuries. In addition, height has increased in developing countries with improved health conditions. From there, we can connect health (shown by height), education, and wages.

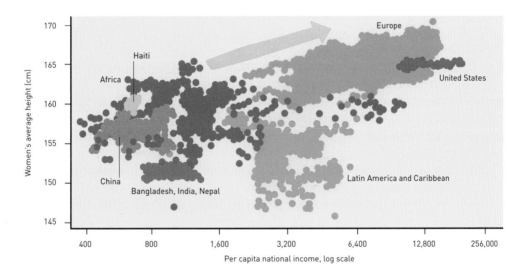

For women, height and income can correlate in some nations.

But not always.

In his book *The Great Escape*, Nobel laureate Angus Deaton demonstrates how things are not quite that simple when it comes to development research. Perhaps proving the height theory, Danish women born in 1980 are much taller than women in Guatemala born in the same year. In higher-income countries we find better sanitation, less childhood disease, and more plentiful diets. However, African populations are often taller, yet poorer, reversing our conclusion. When Deaton concludes that height is not a "sensible measure of wellbeing," he is just reminding us of the human complexities of development economics.

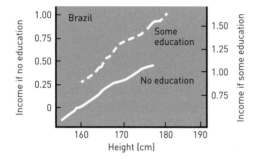
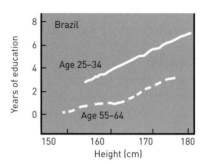

These graphs display the correlation for Brazilian men.

Education

Comparing literacy rates for men and women, we see a gap favoring the former over the latter. And yet women's rate of return from education is higher than men's in lower-income countries. Higher literacy for women—and improved educational attainment in general—leads to later marriage, fewer children, improved childhood nutrition, and greater labor force participation—which leads to greater economic growth for the country as a whole.

One study in Morocco indicated that a mother's health knowledge was "the crucial skill for raising child health." From there, development economists cite the potential spillover from school performance to what an educated person shares with the people around her. The mother's health knowledge spills over to her family and neighbors. And from there it ripples further.

To understand why literacy rates are lower in developing nations, we must first understand the respective private and social costs and benefits of education. As you might expect, private cost refers to what the individual and her household or business sacrifice, while the social costs and benefits measure its impacts on society as a community or a country.

With education, from the family's perspective, it is costly to lose children's labor by sending them to school. However, over the years, the benefit to the individual and the household grows. Correspondingly, for society, education is an expense. Our view as economists takes us to the margin. On a private level, even for primary school, the returns from education exceed its costs. Publicly too, we need to decide the dividing line where an extra year of education has a sufficient return.

Literacy rate in adult men, 2021

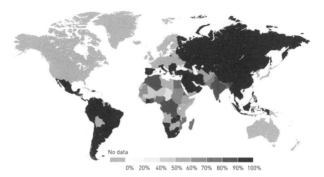

Especially in Africa's lower-income countries, adult women's literacy rates can average below 50 percent, while men's tend to exceed 50 percent.

Literacy rate in adult women, 2021

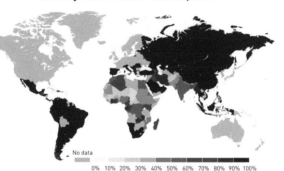

PRIVATE BENEFIT ▶ *as compared to a social benefit, the ways in which a decision, an event, or a contract elevates the status of an individual, a household, or a business.*

SOCIAL BENEFIT ▶ *as compared to the private benefit, the ways in which a decision, an event, or a contracts elevate the status of a geographical region or a country.*

PRIVATE COST ▶ *as compared to the social cost, the sacrifices that a decision, an event, or a contract creates for smaller units such as households and businesses.*

SOCIAL COST ▶ *as compared to the private cost, the sacrifices that a decision, an event, or a contract creates for a community or a nation.*

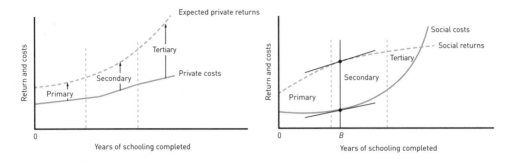

In the left graph, the private benefit of education rises through the tertiary stage. In the right graph, social benefit slows and social costs rise after primary education as shown by the line drawn at B.

Whereas a graph of the private and social costs and benefits of education illustrates the big idea, it does not show us some of the realities. At the primary level, we might find rural schools in low-income nations with one textbook for as many as five students. Children in South Asia can complete primary school without learning to read. Once we get to tertiary education, we should note that the highest subsidies go to the elites. And yet there, too, we see an inequality that location reveals. With elite universities in just one or two cities in developing nations, they remain accessible to a select few in those cities—exacerbating a gap that already exists between rural and urban incomes.

DEBT

Our snapshot of selected development topics would be incomplete without some financial questions and answers. They will involve what developing nations borrow and small business finance.

Countries

Unsurprisingly, developing nations often borrow money for projects and international obligations. They need to fund infrastructure projects such as electrification and road building. Then, on the financial side, they need loans to alleviate balance of payments shortfalls, including not having enough foreign exchange reserves to pay for imports. Also, they might have insufficient funds to service their debt obligations.

To secure funds, their first stop could be an international organization like the World Bank or the IMF (International Monetary Fund). The World Bank and the IMF were established in 1944 at the Bretton Woods Conference in New Hampshire. After World War II ended, the two organizations were supposed to help the world rebuild. The goal was a revitalized financial system. The focus of the IMF was balance-of-payments needs. In other words, it was there to offset emergencies caused by an inability to pay debt or import obligations. Now it has outstanding lending arrangements with more than 80 countries, including $16.1 billion to 49 low-income countries. Meanwhile, the World Bank has evolved from an institution that focused primarily on infrastructure funding to a more recent emphasis on ending extreme poverty in the bottom 40 percent of developing countries' populations.

In addition, it is possible that developing nations will sell bonds to investors that include banks, businesses, countries, individuals, and institutional groups such as pension funds. Rising interest rates could become a problem when they increase the cost of borrowing.

Foreign Aid

Defined as the international transfer of funds or resources, foreign aid also targets inequality with a loan or a grant. Satisfying those criteria, the World Bank and IMF loans would be called foreign aid. So too are official grants and technical assistance. Also defined as foreign aid, we can include any projects that receive specific factors of production or more generic funding from abroad.

While foreign aid is tough to quantify, it does have two criteria:

1. The donor should define the transfer as noncommercial.
2. A loan should be characterized by "concessional terms" that reflect a lower rate than commerce would dictate.

FOREIGN AID ▶ *the international, noncommercial transfer of funds or resources at concessional terms.*

The negative and positive externalities vary considerably too. On the plus side, when there is a political motivation, we can look from the top down and the bottom up at the aid's spillover. Starting with the Marshall Plan through which rebuilding Europe had a massive local impact after World War II, the West also sought to contain Communism. From there, a history of foreign aid could leapfrog from an emphasis on Southeast Asia during the 1960s and Africa and the Persian Gulf in the 1970s. From there, the Caribbean and Central America were foreign aid priorities for the US and then the Russian Federation and the Middle East during the 1990s.

By contrast, the Netherlands, Denmark, Sweden, and Norway have had less of a political motivation fueling their foreign aid. Elsewhere, policies have had an economic motivation, which included increasing the savings rate and the skill rate through technical expertise. It is also possible that nongovernmental organizations (NGOs) provide aid.

At this point, for externalities, as with the aid itself, we can say it is difficult to generalize. Like development assistance, there is a debate about whether aid promotes growth or retards it by substituting domestic initiative with outside help. We also could add questions about whether aid focuses too much on contemporary technology, thereby leaving behind more traditional cultures and exacerbating inequality. All though return us to the local focus that Duflo, Banerjee, and Kremer suggest.

Individuals and Small Businesses

We can begin with a small fruit vendor standing on the street corner in Chennai, India. She has a small cart with some tomatoes that she bought in the morning on credit that she must pay back in the evening. And that is the problem. If it was 1,000 rupees that she owed, the interest would have been more than 4 percent.

Dominated by small-scale enterprises like this vendor, the participants in the business sector of developing nations have little access to traditional finance. Noncorporate and unlicensed, small farmers, artisans, and street vendors typically need small sums, usually less than $1,000, that they traditionally borrow from family or moneylenders at exorbitant rates.

The borrowing–selling–repaying cycle prevented people from saving until microfinance organizations recognized both the problem and the potential profits. Microfinance institutions (MFIs) began to supply credit, saving vehicles, and other kinds of financial services. One recipient of the Nobel Peace Prize, the Bangladeshi entrepreneur Muhammad Yunus, created the Grameen Bank in 1976. Now an established micro-credit institution, Grameen gives small loans to borrowers without requiring collateral; they could be used for a vast menu of financing needs that include livestock, crops, or setting up a very small business known as a microenterprise.

MICROFINANCE ▶ *the financial services that are provided to low-income individuals in small increments.*

HOW MICROFINANCING WORKS

Small loan is made (for buying livestock)

Support group formed and goals identified (livestock are purchased)

Training provided (in animal husbandry, accounting, and business)

Products are sold (milk and eggs from the livestock are sold)

Loan is repaid with interest

But there are alternatives to MFIs, especially peer-to-peer banking and lending groups. Rotating Saving and Credit Associations (ROSCAs) collect savings from groups comprising 50 or fewer members that a leader then allocates on a rotating basis. Members might use a loan to buy a sewing machine. A less obvious benefit is how the funds' limited availability allows married women to block their husbands' access to funds. Esther Duflo tells us about a Kenyan vendor selling beans, sorghum, and maize who belonged to six ROSCAs. Each had a special purpose. The money from one covered her rent, another school fees. To one she contributed 1,000 Kenyan shillings per month; to another, 580 twice a month. She also had shares in a village savings bank that let her borrow a larger sum and build a house. She rejected formal banking processes because of the fees and the cost and inconvenience of travel.

One thing that would have made that Kenyan vendor's banking experience easier was M-PESA. This is a cellphone-based banking service that allows participants to use a phone to pay bills and transfer money. Assume, for example, that a local grocery store is an M-PESA user, or "correspondent." Savers can go to the grocery store to make a deposit that they can send to another correspondent, where a relative or a person to whom they owe money might withdraw it.

The one thread that ties all of our examples together is how new microfinance technology can help small-scale businesses fuel economic growth and development.

M–PESA ▶ *the cellphone-based banking system used primarily by the rural poor who have little access to more formal banking institutions.*

Production Possibilities Graphs

Summarizing development economics, we can return to the production possibilities curves with which we began Chapter 1. We can use them to display economic growth through capital accumulation that covers investments in physical and human capital through better health and education.

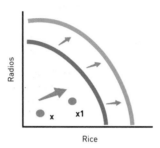

By moving from dots that show underutilization to growth and a new curve, we can see the impact of new physical and human capital.

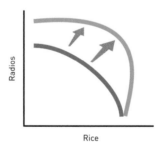

Then, shaped differently, a new curve can show the innovation that spurs technological progress.

And finally, we can also return to the sisters with whom we began. As examples of poverty, of the shift from agriculture to the factory, of unpaid work at home to wage labor, and of traditional rigidity to contemporary flexibility, they humanize development.

They allow us to end where we began. The two sisters were looking for a way to better their lives. And, indeed, focusing on households, communities, and countries, development economics is about how people can do just that.

ECONOMIC GROWTH AND EXTERNALITIES

*Recycling—Externalities—
Economic Growth: Living Standards,
Inequality, and Public Policy—
The Environment*

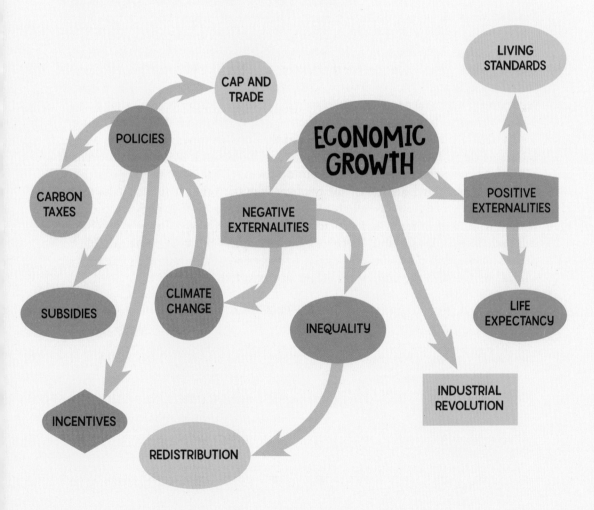

Throughout this book, we've considered supply and demand, fiscal and monetary policy, finance and globalization. Now, for our last step, our focus will be the impact of economic growth and the factors that affect it. By pondering the many sides of growth, we can better understand the past and plan for the future.

RECYCLING

China was once the world's go-to destination for plastic waste. It needed the material for its factories, so that it could be recycled into food cartons, water bottles, artificial plants, clothing, and all manner of other synthetic products. It was a win-win for everybody: China got cheap raw materials to work with and the rest of the world got to export its garbage overseas. Unfortunately, this was not such a great solution for the planet. Much of the plastic China accepted ended up in landfill sites or on towering mountains of waste—or, when it was repurposed into new products, underwent a manufacturing process that was so polluting that it became counterproductive and environmentally devastating.

By 2021, China had stopped taking in the world's unwanted plastic waste. It did not do this for entirely "green" reasons, however. It stopped its recycling activities because it no longer needed to do them; China's economic growth by the start of the third decade of the century was such that it was able to focus its commercial activities elsewhere. What this meant for other nations, though, was that they no longer had a place to dump their trash. Other states soon stepped up—Malaysia and Vietnam, for example—but they were unable to process unwanted plastic as efficiently, in the same volumes, and as cheaply as China. As a result, the cost of recycling skyrocketed.

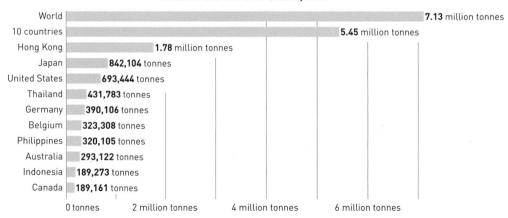

PLASTIC EXPORTS TO CHINA, 2016

World	7.13 million tonnes
10 countries	5.45 million tonnes
Hong Kong	1.78 million tonnes
Japan	842,104 tonnes
United States	693,444 tonnes
Thailand	431,783 tonnes
Germany	390,106 tonnes
Belgium	323,308 tonnes
Philippines	320,105 tonnes
Australia	293,122 tonnes
Indonesia	189,273 tonnes
Canada	189,161 tonnes

0 tonnes   2 million tonnes   4 million tonnes   6 million tonnes

The effect of this reverberated around the world. In the US, for example, municipalities that had been selling their recyclables to China now had to pay for them to be taken away. Once a source of income, plastic waste became a new expense and the target of new programs.

In some communities in Maine, where households had bought their own trash bags, residents wound up having to pay more for them—as much as $2 for a 30-gallon bag. The good news was that the city received $1.65 for every sale, adding to its revenue. The bad news was the extra $200 or so a year each household would have to spend on the bags. Because of China's decision to stop importing waste, Maine's residents felt the impact.

The program, called pay-as-you-throw, reduced each municipality's spending on trash collection. Without the program, trash disposal spending was as much as $120 a ton. Happily, by incentivizing residents to throw out less, pay-as-you-throw programs halved waste tonnages. At the same time, the waste that was collected provided a revenue stream for local authorities. One small city, for example, reported that after a year or so, pay-as-you-throw taxes had added $432,000 to its bottom line.

Plastic waste is loaded onto a container ship.

ECONOMIC GROWTH ▶ *the increase in goods and services represented by a higher real GDP compared to a previous time period.*

The spillover benefits of the economic growth it was experiencing elsewhere in its economy was one reason China was able to stop taking in plastic waste. Defined as the impact that a policy, contract, or decision creates, spillover can be divided into the positive and negative externalities that will be our start point for investigating the impact of economic growth. It will take us to our living standards, to equality, and to public policy.

SPILLOVER ▶ *the ripple effect created by a policy, contract, or decision.*

EXTERNALITIES

To consider how our actions can sometimes unknowingly affect others, think of an apartment building where one resident decides to practice playing his trombone into the early hours of the morning, resulting in a sleepless night for another resident and a poor result on the exam they had to take that day. Or there's that person at the football stadium who unfurls a large banner just as the game starts, meaning that those sitting behind it cannot see the action on the field. We can even think of the decision we make to leave for work at a certain time each morning, and whether we contribute to traffic and transport delays by setting off at the same time as everybody else. In each example, the action results in a negative externality.

However, it works just as powerfully the other way, too. If I mow my lawn regularly and keep my house looking presentable, my neighbor will receive a higher price when she comes to sell her home. When a profitable business contributes more income to a town's tax revenues, it could result in the local police station acquiring a new computer that allows law enforcement officers to work more efficiently to both solve and prevent more crimes. Similarly, you initiate the ripple of a positive externality by getting your annual flu shot.

As we first saw in Chapter 3, an externality is the impact of an agreement or a decision on a bystander. We've also called it a market failure, because the initial act had insufficiently appropriate incentives. When a negative externality is the result, the cost of the initial act or decision should have been higher. Correspondingly, a positive ripple had more of a benefit than the market recognized. For each, equilibrium was in the wrong place. It was either too low, incentivizing more of the harmful behavior, or too high, encouraging less.

Externalities provide the lens through which we will conclude our introduction to economics. Through externalities, we will look at the global and local wonders and dangers of economic growth. By looking at the past and present, we can start to contemplate the future.

ECONOMIC GROWTH: LIVING STANDARDS, INEQUALITY, AND PUBLIC POLICY

Economic growth elevated our living standards. However, as Nobel laureate Angus Deaton told us in Chapter 11, it also inevitably created inequality. But it took a while for both to emerge.

Living Standards

Going back in time to our hunter-gatherer ancestors, we would have seen that they habitually ate most if not all of the food they captured or foraged for each day. Each morning, they had to begin their daily search for food anew.

Then, around 12,000 years ago, humans learned how to farm. This allowed them to settle in one place, and to grow crops and raise livestock. It allowed them to divide the present from the future and start to make plans, to store and preserve what they did not immediately consume, and to develop ways to produce more of the foodstuffs they needed. Life became safer, healthier, and more stable.

Looking back to the early 19th century and before, we would have seen a world far poorer than today's. Then the world, though not equally, became more affluent. Between 1820 and 2020 we would have seen a 15-fold increase in the world's average per capita GDP.

Agriculture

Agricultural productivity helped to elevate our living standards. Fast-forwarding from the earliest farmers to the 1800s, we see immense changes in a farmer's land, labor, and capital. We learned to rotate crops and developed equipment that expedited planting and harvesting. Simple but effective solutions to everyday problems had far-reaching consequences. Planting hedgerows, for example, protected exposed fields from the erosive effects of wind—and helped to keep roving cattle and hungry wildlife away from vulnerable crops. Meanwhile, transportation networks facilitated the regional specialization that could optimize output. In the US, the South could plant cotton, the North could manufacture textiles, and the West could feed everyone with the grains it grew.

The ultimate result, skipping ahead to now, was an immense increase in output. In the US, from 1948 to 2017, farm productivity tripled. Looking closely at the increase, we would have seen less labor and less land, more than offset by human capital and technology. Increases in human capital led to genetically modified seeds. Farm capital meant new equipment such as harvesters that not only replaced people but could perform multiple different functions, quickly and efficiently.

Technology

Again, looking back, we would have seen farm productivity boost industry's factors of production. Able to feed more than the people that populated their communities, farmers could send food to the city. With productivity growing and technological advances meaning they were no longer needed to work the land, people moved from the farm to the factory. Many were living longer. Urban populations grew. We had an Industrial Revolution that displayed the power of the machine.

However, growth did not occur equally and at the same rate everywhere. After ascending until 1600, Spain's economy stalled as Great Britain's soared. Similarly, Argentina had been one of the world's richest countries in 1900, but its growth plateaued thereafter. By contrast, robust postwar growth in Japan and South Korea has placed their populations near the top of world wealth lists. In Europe, from 1950 to 1973, GDP per capita increased by 3.8 percent every year. After that, though, it appears to have slowed down.

Looking at the positive externalities of past growth, we can go straight to the home and the factory and echo what we said in Chapter 3. At home, technology saved time and enabled women to join the labor force. It increased literacy and health. At work, through the power of the machine, productivity rose.

Light was a cause and effect of growth. Using a measure of brightness called the lumen as one of his metrics, and the pay for a day's labor as the other, Nobel economics laureate William Nordhaus observed that less and less work paid for more and more light. Whereas in ancient Babylon you had to work for a day to be able to afford just 10 minutes of light, by the 19th century that same day's labor could purchase you five hours' worth of light through a kerosene lamp. And astoundingly, by the 1990s, the amount of light you could afford from a day's work soared to 20,000 hours. Using light as an example of a positive externality, we could begin with being able to light up our homes at night and end with the safety that streetlights bring us. When we eliminated our

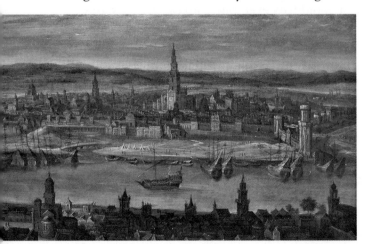

dependence on natural light we became less concerned about positioning windows, and this allowed us to build our homes differently. Light let us add substantially to the human capital that propelled growth.

A view of Seville in 1580. In the 16th century, Spain was one of the wealthiest countries in the world.

Inequality

Life Expectancy

In addition, the unequal life expectancy created by growth is an externality. A life expectancy of 30 to 40 years was probably typical more than 200 years ago; now, in the UK, for example, it is close to 80. As recently as 1950, life expectancy was just 35.6 years in South Korea. Today, having experienced an intense growth spurt, a South Korean born in 2019 can expect to live to 83.

For the individual, the family, and the country, the positive externalities of the economic growth experienced by higher-income countries through longer, healthier lives range from the concrete impact of longer labor force participation to the abstract structure and support of multiple generations of a family. The externalities could also relate to the lower birth rates that economists hypothesize will result after a larger elderly cohort initially boosts population. In addition to life expectancy, surveys have indicated that a higher GDP correlates with life satisfaction, better education, and lower infant mortality rates.

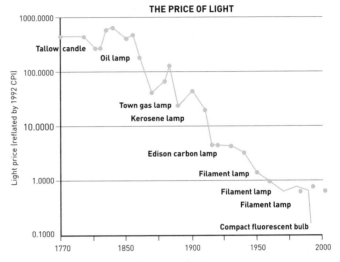

The downward march of the price of light.

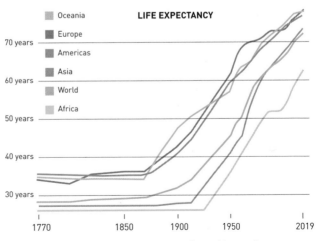

Growing everywhere, life expectancy reflected inequality.

But we are only looking at a part of the world. Small differences in annual growth rates compounded to create the negative externality of global inequality. Whereas the average annual growth rate of Western Europe between 1820 and 2010 was 1.4 percent, for Africa it was closer to 0.8 percent. The result was an ever-increasing gap that reflected a doubling growth rate for Africa while that of the West quadrupled. Consequently, at close to 63 years, the average African's life expectancy is considerably less than that of people in higher-income regions.

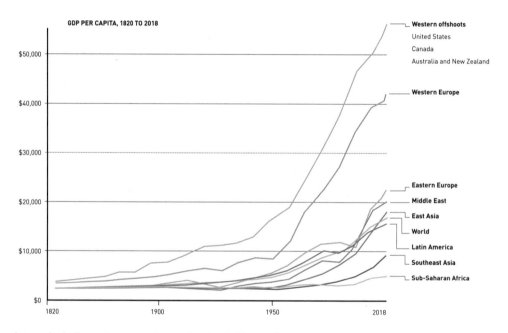

Increasingly disparate economic growth rates fed inequality.

Public Policy
Redistribution

Public policy can diminish health and wealth inequalities that result from disparate economic growth. Within a country, through taxation, redistribution can shift money from those who have more to those who have less. Governments can use that tax revenue for tertiary education, or for healthcare and eldercare. Sometimes called social protection, entitlement spending varies from country to country, as shown in the table opposite. It can also vary within countries. In the US, affluent California spends much more on entitlements than less well-off Mississippi.

REDISTRIBUTION ▶ *as it relates to fiscal policy, the decision to take money from one group and spend it on another one.*

	Social Expenditure as a % of GDP (2016)	Average Tax Rate (2017)
US	19.3%	31.7%
Portugal	24.1%	41.4%
France	31.5%	47.6%

THE ENVIRONMENT

Continuing with the externalities of growth, our last stop is the environment. Simply defined, environmental economics takes us to how economic activity affects the natural environment. Although pollution will be our main focus, we could consider too how we extract minerals, our treatment of marine life, our land use, and our energy extraction methods. We also could look at water and agriculture.

To mitigate global warming, the goal is an increase of no more than 1.5°C (2.7°F). To achieve this, we would need to reduce CO_2 emissions by 45 percent from 2010 to 2030 and reach net zero by 2050. Even then, projections suggests that 70 percent of all coral reefs would still perish. Reducing emissions returns us to economic growth. In his 2018 Nobel Prize lecture, economist William Nordhaus demonstrated the environmental cost of economic growth through a simple graphic (below right).

We also can look at production possibilities graphs. On an environmental production possibilities graph, our y-axis represents the goods and services that an economy produces. It could be cars and computers, loaves of bread and dental examinations—any pair. Then, representing environmental quality, the x-axis embodies a broad range of variables that would include water quality, urban noise, and the sulfur dioxide emissions that reflect ambient quality— the quantity of pollutants in the environment. One concern is that the environmental degradation created by economic growth could reverse its trajectory: more growth could ultimately lead to less growth.

? Economic growth leads to CO_2 emissions

Rising CO_2 concentration and other forces lead to climate change

Climate change imposes ecological and economic impacts

? Climate change policies reduce emissions

Also returning to basic economic concepts, we can ask about the supply curve. At this point market failure enters the picture. Because the position of the supply curve ignored the social cost of pollution, producers will create more than an optimal amount. Shown here, you can see the gap between the private firm's supply curve and what would be good for all of us.

We could compare the overproducing typical firm to our driving behavior. When we drive a fossil-fuel-powered car, we create emissions and congestion. Because we are using an open access resource—a resource everyone can use—we use the road with little thought about environmental externalities. Because there is an inadequate cost, we excessively use our roads.

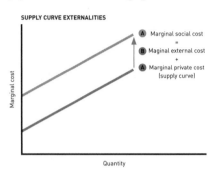

SUPPLY CURVE EXTERNALITIES

A Marginal social cost
=
B Maginal external cost
+
A Marginal private cost
(supply curve)

Marginal cost

Quantity

If a firm had to pay a social cost, its supply would decrease.

COMMON POOL RESOURCES (CPR) ▶ an open access environment that makes it difficult to block use and therefore easy to overuse.

We also create a second externality that has another meaning beyond driving. Assume for example that with 10, 20, or 30 cars on the road, travel time is 10 minutes. However, 50 cars will raise the travel time to 12 minutes; 80 cars to 24 minutes. The big idea is that, alone, we have minimal impact. Together, we ruin it for everyone. So too with the environment, as all of our behaviors converge within one polluted pathway that supply curves need to recognize.

This is one example of what economists term the "tragedy of the commons." The "commons" refers to the resources that "belong" to all of us rather than being owned by one individual or group or business. Ever since the commons was analyzed by the American ecologist Garrett Hardin in 1968, most economists have assumed that we have no incentive to conserve the number of fish in our oceans or to ensure the cleanliness of our air. Similarly, if a community uses a local pasture run by the town, residents have no reason to minimize what their livestock consume. The conclusion was that commonly possessed commodities will be abused and overused because there are no incentives to preserve them as there are in the private sector. As a result, it was thought, government or private ownership are the only alternatives.

TRAGEDY OF THE COMMONS ▶ *when resources are abused and overused because they are "owned" by society rather than an individual.*

All that we consume—the goods and services on which economic growth depends—requires the energy that creates emissions. We could direct our attention to where the goods are made, which would take us to lower- and middle-income countries mainly located in Asia. But we also need to look at where many of those goods and services are used: the richer countries.

If we agree that someone, somewhere has to pay the cost of reducing emissions, the question is, who?

On an individual basis, behavioral economists tell us that we value the present more than the future. For that reason, many of us are unwilling to make the current sacrifices that would make the world a better place later. Plus, consciously or otherwise, we do not always make the connection between our demand for goods and services and the emissions that are created "over there" in some distant location to fulfil them.

On a national basis, public policies also create different incentives. Using a command approach, a government can say to firms that they cannot pollute, and the result would be a penalty if they did. They would be returning us to Arthur Pigou and his Pigovian solutions from Chapter 3. As we have seen, they benefit society in two ways. They stop a negative externality and, while doing so, they can generate revenue.

The big problem here is that policy makers are not thinking at the margin. Deciding where marginal cost and marginal benefit equal each other would have been more beneficial for society rather than entirely eliminating the behavior that created the externality. We don't want the cost of prevention to exceed its benefit.

Carbon Taxes

CLIMATE CHANGE POLICIES

Subsidies

Cap-and-trade schemes

Regulations

A second possibility called cap and trade takes us to the market. This is a policy that creates pollution permits which firms can sell to each other through a central market. First, government establishes a maximum amount of pollution—a cap. Then firms that are below the cap can sell the right to pollute to others that are above it. The EU calls its Emissions Trading System a cornerstone for reducing greenhouse gas emissions. The EU has the world's first carbon market and the largest one.

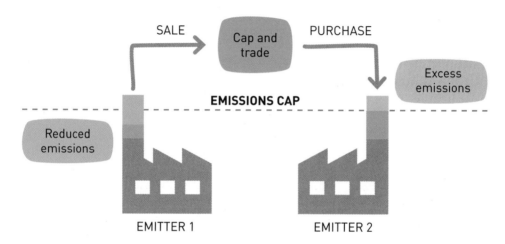

How cap and trade works.

Yet another approach is the carbon tax. When producers have to pay a tax for the carbon emissions generated by the goods and services they create, they decide for themselves what the costs and benefits are. They weigh the cost of the tax against the benefits of doing nothing, and when the marginal costs exceed the marginal benefits, the firm will stop emitting. An economist might point out that a firm—more knowledgeable about its own business than the government—would make the most productive decision about how much to emit.

From national mitigation, we can move to global inequality. With middle-income countries becoming increasingly affluent, more people can enjoy the amenities of growth. However, as they narrow the global inequality gap, they create more emissions.

Take air conditioning.

Enjoying the benefits of an average annual 6.9 percent growth rate from 2000 to 2019, a typical bank employee in India could afford to run the air conditioner that she needed every day during the summer of 2022 when temperatures exceeded all-time highs of 117°F (47.2°C). Quite simply, it was too hot to work. Some towns opened their schools for just three hours a day and canceled sports events. Crops shriveled in their fields and productivity in factories and workshops plunged. In a typical Indian factory, every degree Celsius above 27°C (80.6°F) results in a 2 percent drop in efficiency. Another study concluded that when the climate becomes 1 percent warmer, per capita income in poorer countries will fall by 1.4 percent.

In these lower per capita income countries, it could seem that air conditioning (AC) makes total sense. Multiplying that one individual by millions, we get soaring AC use in a warming world. Knowing that many people are more comfortable and healthier, we can see the positive externalities of growth.

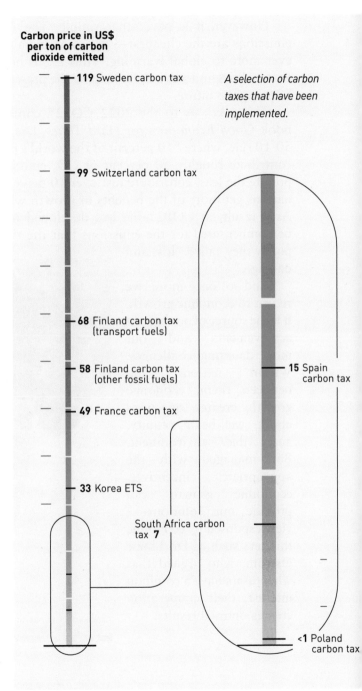

Carbon price in US$ per ton of carbon dioxide emitted

119 Sweden carbon tax

A selection of carbon taxes that have been implemented.

99 Switzerland carbon tax

68 Finland carbon tax (transport fuels)

58 Finland carbon tax (other fossil fuels)

49 France carbon tax

15 Spain carbon tax

33 Korea ETS

South Africa carbon tax 7

<1 Poland carbon tax

However, it is never that simple. The AC units that have the highest emissions are the cheapest—and so as India's economy grows, it contributes ever more to global warming. Thus AC is both a cure for growth's negative externalities and a cause. By helping the present with economic growth, we are harming the future.

This takes us to the 2022 COP27 climate change conference. In their book *Good Economics for Hard Times*, Drs. Duflo and Banerjee outline the 50-10 rule, where "10 percent of the world's population (the highest polluters) contribute roughly 50 percent of CO_2 emissions, while the 50 percent who pollute the least contribute just over 10 percent." Correspondingly, the richer nations get more of the benefits of growth while poorer nations feel the cost. As a result, at COP27 the less developed nations argued that they should be compensated for the emissions that the richer nations created, through a policy they called "loss and damage."

And so, once more, we return to economic growth. It is the source of our biggest achievements and our most daunting challenges. Within nations and between them, economic growth creates questions about well-being, equity, and the environment. But managed with the appropriate incentives, economic growth can provide our solutions—a view espoused by economic thinkers such as Dr. Elinor Ostrom, who argued that when users have a common interest, their cooperation creates optimal results.

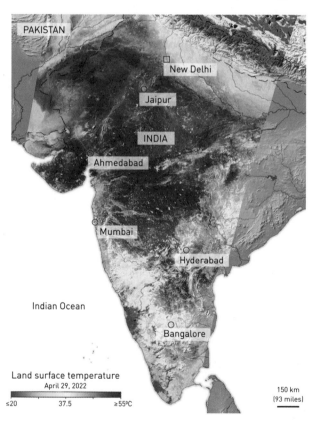

A satellite image showing the heatwave across India in April 2022.

GLOSSARY

Absolute Advantage: an economic principle that says one geographic area has the ability to produce a good or service more efficiently than another geographic area.

Aggregate Demand (AD) Curve: on a graph, the representation of the quantity of goods and services that consumers, businesses, government, and people from abroad are willing and able to spend at each price level.

Aggregate Supply (AS) Curve: on a graph, the representation of the quantity of goods and services that firms produce and sell at each price level.

Behavioral Economics: the field of economics that includes psychology; behavioral economists say we have a human, more unpredictable dimension.

Bills: similar to bonds and notes, bills are government IOUs that mature in 4 to 52 weeks and pay interest.

Bond: a debt obligation from a government or a business firm. Government bonds typically pay interest and mature after 10 years.

Choice Architecture: from behavioral economics; like the design of a building where placement of the doors and stairs affect where people walk, so too are our decisions affected by the structure within which we make them.

Circular Flow Model: a simplified illustration showing where money, goods, services, and the factors of production move in an economic system.

Command: a top-down economic system through which one person or group of people answer the three basic economic questions that determine production and distribution.

Commercial Bank: a financial intermediary that connects savers and borrowers through pools of savings created by deposits and loans to businesses and households.

Common Pool Resources (CPR): an open access environment that makes it difficult to block use and therefore easy to overuse.

Comparative Advantage: an economic principle that suggests the world will get the highest gains from trade when each nation produces the goods and services for which it has the lowest opportunity cost.

Competitive Market Structures: the markets in which businesses compete that are each characterized by more or less power for the firm.

Concentration Ratio: the proportion of market share that belongs to the largest two to eight firms in a market. Higher numbers, indicating more concentration and market dominance by large firms, reflect less competition.

Consumption Expenditures: the GDP component that totals the money value of the goods and services on which households spend.

Cost: sacrifice; the sacrifice(s) created by a decision because of what was not selected.

Cyclical Unemployment: the temporary joblessness caused by the downward spiral of the business cycle.

Debt: the total amount that the federal government owes.

Deficit: the amount by which government spending exceeds government revenue during one fiscal year.

Demand: the different price/quantity pairs at which a consumer is willing and able to buy goods and services.

Depreciation: when, over time, the value of a capital good loses some value. The difference between GDP and NDP.

Derivative: a security whose value is based on other securities.

Development Economics: the study of how the incomes, the human capital, and the power of people in lower-income countries can increase.

Development Plan: a blueprint for changing an economic system in order to propel the growth that will elevate well-being.

Discretionary Expenditures: the optional federal budget spending that is not required by law.

Double Entry Bookkeeping: a business's accounting records that include its assets and liabilities.

Dual Mandate: as determined by the U.S. Congress, the main two goals of the U.S. Federal Reserve are low, stable prices and maximum sustainable employment.

Durable Goods: goods that have an average life of more than three years.

Economic Growth: compared to a previous time period, the increase in the money value of goods and services that are produced, represented by a higher real GDP.

Economics: the study of the production and distribution of "scarce" land, labor, and capital.

Economies of Scale: the lower cost per item created by big firms when they produce large quantities of goods.

Elasticity: the extent to which a change in price affects a change in quantity demanded.

Entitlement Spending: money spent on programs that populations expect government will provide. Examples in the United States are Medicare and Social Security.

Entitlements: federal budget items that many people expect the government will provide, like healthcare.

Entrepreneur: the innovator that propels economic growth by creating new businesses that become new industries.

Equation of Exchange: Stated as MV=PQ, an equation that displays the influence of the money supply on output when the velocity of money is relatively stable.

Equilibrium: the price and quantity at which the quantity supplied and the quantity demanded are equal.

Exports: the goods and services that are produced domestically, and then sent and (potentially) sold outside that country.

Externality: the positive or negative impact of a contract or decision as it ripples beyond its original source to unrelated bystanders.

Extreme Poverty: defined by income as living beneath the World Bank's $2.15 poverty line, but also including intangibles like lack of prestige and power.

Factor Markets: the markets in which the price and quantity of land, labor, and capital—the factors of production—are determined through supply and demand.

Factors of Production: the land, labor, and capital from which all goods and services are made.

Financial Intermediary: an institution that enables savers and borrowers to interact.

Fiscal Policy: a government's spending, taxing, and borrowing.

Foreign Aid: the international transfer of funds or resources.

Friction: a financial transaction cost that, as in physics, diminishes speed.

Frictional Unemployment: the joblessness that we always experience for the everyday reasons that people leave jobs.

Gains from Trade: the benefits from exchanging goods and services when participants get more than they previously had.

Gini Coefficient: a number that displays income or wealth inequality.

Globalization: closer economic, cultural, and political ties among countries.

Gross Domestic Product (GDP): the money value of the final goods and services produced in a specified geographical area (typically a country) during a specific time period (usually a year).

Gross Investment: the GDP component whose main parts are the money value of the plant, equipment, and software that businesses use and also (somewhat surprisingly) residential housing.

Gross National Product (GNP): the money value of the final goods and services produced by a country within and beyond its borders during a specific time period (usually a year).

Hedge Fund: a financial fund that is actively managed through varied investing approaches.

Herfindahl-Hirschman Index (HHI): an index number that indicates the concentration among the firms in a market. Higher numbers, usually above 2,500, indicate highly concentrated less competitive markets while 1,500 or less signals more competition.

Imports: the goods and services that are produced outside of a nation and then sent and (potentially) sold inside that country.

Increasing Returns to Scale: when less or the same input creates more output because of the synergy between mass production and technological progress.

Index Fund: a financial fund that is composed of many securities, usually from a certain category.

Inferior Goods: the lower-quality goods and services that we are willing and able to purchase less of when our income rises and more of when it falls.

Information Asymmetry: a transaction situation in which one party knows more than the other.

Investment Bank: a financial intermediary that connects savers and borrowers by enabling individuals, businesses, and municipalities to provide and access money through securities.

Labor Markets: the process that determines the number of jobs and what workers are paid.

Liquidity: the ease with which a security can be traded for cash.

M-PESA: the mobile phone-based banking system used primarily by the rural poor who have little access to more formal banking institutions.

Macroeconomics: the study of economics through a big issue lens that would include an entire nation's monetary (money supply and credit) and fiscal (spending, taxing, and borrowing) policies.

Mandatory Expenditures: dominating the US federal budget, the categories of fiscal policy spending that are required by law.

Marginal: the last extra item or amount. Marginal cost is the extra cost of the one extra unit that was produced. Marginal utility is the extra satisfaction or usefulness created by one extra worker or one extra hour of study.

Market: a bottom-up economic system through which many people and businesses give the answers to the three economic questions that determine production and distribution by responding to supply and demand incentives.

Market Failure: when the market's equilibrium price inadequately reflects the cost of societal cost or benefit.

Microeconomics: the study of economics from the bottom up that would include household supply and demand and how individual business firms behave.

Microfinance: the financial services that are provided to low-income individuals in small increments.

Mixed Economy: an economic system that combines the characteristics of tradition, command, and/or the market.

Monetary Policy: Overseen by central banks, monetary policy targets the supply of money and credit in an economy.

Money: any commodity that serves as a medium of exchange, a unit of value, and a store of value.

Money Multiplier: the number that shows how many times the reserves created by a deposit increase the money supply when they move through the banking system as a succession of deposits and loans.

Monopolistic Competition: a market composed of many firms and many consumers. Firms engaging monopolistic competition range from small to somewhat large, they have some pricing power, their products are similar and yet unique, and they can enter and exit the market relatively easily. Monopolistic Competition is one of the four basic competitive market structures.

Monopoly: a market composed of one firm and many consumers. Monopolies are usually quite large, and, as price makers, they have considerable pricing power. It is almost impossible to enter a market dominated by a monopoly. Monopoly is one of the four basic competitive market structures.

Moral Hazard: an attitude that is created when the downside of risk is minimized, thereby creating the incentive to take on more risk.

Mutual Fund: an investing vehicle that makes shares of a diverse portfolio available to small and large buyers.

Nationalization: the process through which the ownership of privately owned property is transferred to government.

Natural Monopoly: a monopoly that lets the market avoid wasteful duplication and thereby is viewed somewhat favorably.

Negative Externality: the harmful impact on an unrelated bystander of an agreement or a decision.

Net Investment: Gross investment minus depreciation.

Net National Product (NDP): the GDP minus depreciation (aka capital consumption).

Non-Durable Goods: the goods we expect to last for fewer than three years.

Non-Institutionalized Population: referred to when calculating the size of the labor force. The non-institutionalized population includes individuals who are not in the military, jail, nursing homes, and other similar kinds of institutions that can be included as a part of the labor force.

Normal Goods: the goods and services that we are willing and able to purchase more of when our income rises and less when it falls. Most everyday items are normal goods and services.

Notes: similar to bonds and bills, notes are government IOUs that mature in two to ten years and pay interest.

Oligopoly: a market composed of few firms and many consumers. Firms in oligopolistic markets are quite large, and, as price makers, they have pricing power, their products can be differentiated or similar, and market entry and exit are difficult. Oligopoly is one of the four basic competitive market structures.

Opportunity Cost: a decision's opportunity cost is its one sacrificed alternative. The opportunity cost is what you might have done.

Option: a contract that gives the buyer the right to purchase or sell different kinds of securities at another time for a pre-determined price.

Pareto Efficiency: when any further allocation of a good or a service will make someone worse off if someone else becomes better off.

Participation Rate: The fraction that compares the entire non-institutionalized population (denominator) to the number of workers in the labor force.

Pay-as-you-go: as with U.S. Social Security, when current tax revenue goes directly to current benefit recipients.

Per Capita GDP: a ratio that divides GDP by population.

Perfect Competition: a market composed of many firms and many consumers. Firms engaging in markets that resemble perfect competition are small, they are price takers, their products are almost identical, and they can enter and enter the market relatively easily. Perfect competition is one of the four basic competitive market structures.

Positive Externality: the good impact on an unrelated bystander of an agreement or a decision.

Poverty Trap: the plight of certain poor households through which they cannot move beyond poverty because of an interwoven cycle whereby one dimension of their lives pulls all others down.

Price: the main source of information from the market.

Price Ceiling: typically mandated by government, a maximum price for a good or service that is below equilibrium.

Price Floor: typically mandated by government, a minimum price for a good or service that is above equilibrium.

Private Benefit: as compared to the social benefit, the ways in which a decision, an event, or a contract adds value to a household or a business.

Private Cost: as compared to the social cost, the sacrifices that a decision, an event, or a contract create for smaller units like households and businesses.

Privatization: the process through which private individuals and businesses purchase state-owned enterprises.

Product Markets: the markets in which the price and quantity of goods and services are determined through supply and demand.

Productivity: the output produced per each unit of labor input.

Quotas: limited quantities, as of imports, established by a government.

Recession: a contraction in economic activity for more than several months that has significant "depth, diffusion, and/or duration."

Redistribution: as it relates to fiscal policy, the decision to take money from one group and then spend it on another one.

Rent: as defined economically, the amount added to the price of land because lower-quality land has become more valuable.

ROSCA (Rotating Savings and Credit Association): groups formed by villagers without easy access to formal banking institutions in developing nations, composed of 50 or fewer people, through which money is pooled and then loaned to members.

Scarcity: limited quantities; the basic economic problem that says the supply of all goods and services is limited.

Schedule: the table or menu that lists price quantity pairs for a demand or supply curve.

Seasonal Unemployment: the jobless numbers that rise and fall as seasons change and holidays come and go.

Securities: including stocks and bonds, financial instruments we can buy and sell that represent value.

Selling Short: an investing style that is successful when price goes down because securities are sold before they are purchased. When investors sell short, they borrow securities, sell those securities, then purchase those securities, and return them to a lender.

Shadow Economy: activities excluded from the GDP that are typically all or partially illegal because revenue or factor payments are not reported.

Social Benefit: as compared to the private benefit, the ways in which a decision, an event, or a contract add value to communities.

Social Cost: as compared to the private cost, the sacrifices that a decision, an event, or a contract create for a community or a nation.

Spillover: composed of positive and negative externalities, the ripple of impact that a policy, contract, or decision creates.

Standard of Living: in addition to or instead of per capita GDP, a metric that measures well-being by looking at work-leisure balance, happiness, and other intangibles.

Stock: securities that are representations of shares of ownership of a corporation. One person, many people, and businesses can own all, some, or a small proportion of the shares of a corporation.

Structural Unemployment: the joblessness and need for new skills in an economy caused by major changes such as new technology.

Subsidies: when given by a government, the money directly or indirectly received by a producer of a good or a service to offset an insufficient market price.

Supply: the different price/quantity pairs at which a producer is willing and able to sell goods and services.

Tariffs: taxes on imports.

Tradition: an economic system that passes down from generation to generation the answers to the three basic economic questions about production and distribution.

Tragedy of the Commons: when resources are abused and overused because they are "owned" by society rather than an individual.

Transfer Payment: money disbursed by government to individuals because of circumstance rather than as a payment for a good or a service; government payments including the UK State Pension and U.S. Social Security.

Unemployment Rate: the fraction that compares the number of people in the labor force (denominator) to the people in the labor force that have no job but are looking for one.

Utility: the usefulness or satisfaction that a good or a service or an event provides to its user.

World Price: the equilibrium price determined by supply and demand in world markets for goods and services.

SUGGESTED READING, PODCASTS, AND VIDEOS

Textbooks

Stevenson, Betsey and Wolfers, Justin (2020) *Principles of Economics*: Worth Publishers Macmillan Learning.
Clear, thorough, and up-to-date, in 895 pages, the Stevenson Wolfers is all you could want from a textbook.

Todaro, Michael P. and Smith, Stephen C. (2020) *Economic Development Thirteenth Edition*: Pearson.
An ideal combination of the human side of development with its numbers. The book includes in-depth country case studies.

General Reading

Buchholz, Todd G. (2021) *New Ideas From Dead Economists 4th Edition*: Penguin Random House LLC.
Devoting each chapter to one or two major economic thinkers, Buchholz humanizes the history of economic thought and conveys its timelessness.

General Audio

Taylor, Timothy (1996) *The Great Courses: Legacies of Great Economists: https://www.thegreatcourses.com/courses/legacies-of-great-economists*
Focusing on one or two economic thinkers in each episode, Professor Taylor is expert at making the people and the ideas come alive.

General Video

https://www.learner.org/series/economics-ua-21st-century-edition/
Composed of 30 episodes, in each video *Economics USA* covers one economic idea through three case studies that are paired with economic explanations.

Chapter 1
Trade-Offs and Margins

Books

Graeber, David and Wengrow, David (2021) *The Dawn of Everything: A New History of Humanity*: Farrar, Straus and Giroux.
This is the ideal introduction to contemporary economies. Taking us from the Ice Age to the earliest states, Graeber and Wengrow present a 704-page historical narrative that says far more about the character and complexity of past cultures than traditional histories.

Roth, Alvin E. (2016) *Who Gets What and Why: The New Economics of Matchmaking and Market Design*: Eamon Dolan/Mariner Books.
An explanation from a Nobel laureate of how goods and people ranging from kidneys to physicians can be optimally allocated by tweaking market incentives.

Chapter 2
Economic Systems

Books

Schmemann, Serge (1997) *Echoes of a Native Land: Two Centuries of a Russian Village*: Alfred A. Knopf.
A *NY Times* journalist returns to his ancestral home and documents two centuries of economic change.

Zubok, Vladislav M. (2021) *Collapse: The Fall of the Soviet Union*: Yale University Press.
Personal and yet also scholarly, *Collapse* is a contemporary explanation from a London School of Economics professor of why the Soviet Union unraveled.

Milanovic, Branko (2021) *Capitalism, Alone: The Future of the System That Rules the World*: Belknap Press: An Imprint of Harvard University Press.
The most recent of a series of Milanovic books that illustrate the different forms of capitalism and their impact on global equality.

Chernow, Ron A. (2002) *Alexander Hamilton*: Penguin Press.
The classic and thoroughly enjoyable story of the life of Alexander Hamilton.

Chapter 3
The Market System

Books

Jevons, Marshall (1978) *Murder at the Margin*: Thomas Horton & Daughters.
A murder mystery in which the protagonist, an economics professor, uses supply and demand to free the innocent and identify the killers.

Wapshott, Nicholas (2021) *Samuelson Friedman: The Battle Over the Free Market*: W.W. Norton & Company.
Enlivened by a foundation of anecdotal stories, Wapshott's book looks at how two economic behemoths saw the market differently.

Chapter 4
Businesses

Books

Micklethwait, John and Wooldridge, Adrian (2005) *The Company: A Short History of a Revolutionary Idea*: The Modern Library.
Taking us to a new lens, *The Company* lets us see that the concept of the corporation was a clever innovation that fueled economic growth.

Pendergast, Mark (2013) *For God, Country, and Coca-Cola*: Basic Books.
To see what a business is, what it can do, and how it can grow, the story of Coca-Cola is the ideal prototype.

Chapter 5
Labor

Podcasts

How I Built This (NPR): *https://podcasts.apple.com/us/podcast/how-i-built-this-with-guy-raz/id1150510297*
In each episode, *How I Built This* focuses on an entrepreneur. Ranging from Spanx to 1-800-GOT-JUNK?, the podcast lets listeners learn how familiar businesses began and grew.

Video

American Dream (1990): Directed by Barbara Kopple. The story of a 6-month strike at a Hormel plant in Austin, Minnesota, Barbara Kopple's Academy Award-winning documentary is about much more than a labor dispute. Viewers meet families that disagree, they see the jobs that people do, and they see the solidarity that unions try to build.

American Factory (2019): Directed by Julia Reichert and Steven Bogner.
After a Chinese company moves into a shuttered General Motors plant in Ohio, hopeful workers discover their new jobs are not what they expected in this Academy Award-winning documentary.

Chapter 6
Fiscal Policy

Books

Skidelsky, Robert (2010) *Keynes: A Very Short Introduction*: Oxford Reprint Edition.
All of Skidelsky's books are the gold standard for Maynard Keynes. But if you prefer not to read his multi-volume biography, this book is ideal.

Wapshott, Nicholas (2012) *Keynes Hayek: The Clash That Defined Modern Economics*: W.W. Norton & Company.
Defining contemporary economics, the Wapshott look at Keynes and Hayek frames our economic choices and dilemmas.

Video

Fear the Boom and Bust: *http://www.youtube.com/user/econstories*
Comparing Keynes and Hayek through rap, this musical video is a memorable summary of how they "clash."

Chapter 7
Monetary Policy

Books

Lowenstein, Roger (2016) *America's Bank: The Epic Struggle To Create The Federal Reserve* (2016): Penguin Books.
Through Roger Lowenstein's lens, you will see the creation of the Federal Reserve as a fascinating story.

Chapter 8
Keeping Track

Books
Coyle, Diane (2015) *GDP: A Brief But Affectionate History*: Princeton University Press.
While Coyle's story is brief, it is also comprehensive—the ideal introduction to the GDP.

Harford, Tim (2021) *The Data Detective*: Riverhead Books.
Always wonderfully interesting, Tim Harford's books anchor all data in stories that immediately engage readers.

Chapter 9
The Financial System

Books
Ferguson, Niall (2009) *The Ascent of Money: A Financial History of the World*: Penguin Books.
Telling all you could want to know about money, this book is the way to grasp what money really is and has been.

Siegel, Jeremy (2022) *Stocks for the Long Run: The Definitive Guide to Financial Market & Long-Term Investment Strategy 6th edition*: McGraw Hill.
More than a source of investment strategy, Jeremy Siegel's book is the classic source for learning all you could want to know about stock market history and how markets function.

Podcasts
The Crypto Story by Matt Levine from *Bloomberg Businessweek* Episodes 1–6: https://podcasts. apple.com/us/podcast/ bloomberg-crypto/id1623197303
In six episodes, financial journalist Matt Levine tells all you could want to know about Bitcoin and cryptocurrency. While the series was a part of the Crypto podcast—*Bloomberg's* daily look at the crypto world—it was originally a 40,000 *Bloomberg Businessweek* article.

Video
Money Man: The Story of JSG Boggs: https://milestonefilms. com/products/money-man
Watching the documentary *Money Man*, viewers ask what is money when Boggs, an artist, has his work seized by the U.S. government.

Chapter 10
Globalization

Books
Rivoli, Pietra (2014) *The Travels of a T-Shirt in the Global Economy: An Economist Examines the Markets, Power, and Politics of World Trade*: Wiley.
For the details about the travels of a t-shirt, the Rivoli book has the whole story.

Irwin, Douglas A. (2019) *Clashing Over Commerce: A History of US Trade Policy (Markets and Governments in Economic History)*: The University of Chicago Press.
Demonstrating the impact of trade policy on globalization, the Irwin book shifts our attention to government.

Levinson, Marc (2008) *The Box: How the Shipping Container Made the World Smaller and the World Economy Bigger*: Princeton University Press.
Through stories about people and commerce, Marc Levinson makes a box come alive.

Chapter 11
Development Economics

Books
Banerjee Abhijit and Duflo, Esther (2011) *Poor Economics: A Radical Rethinking of the Way to Fight Global Poverty*: Public Affairs.
Nobel laureates Banerjee and Duflo tell the story of their work.

Thaler, Richard H. (2015) *Misbehaving: The Making of Behavioral Economics*: W.W. Norton & Company.
Combining his own history with the evolution of behavioral economics, Thaler's book has two very human captivating stories.

Thaler, Richard H. and Sunstein, Cass R. (2021) *Nudge*: Yale University Press.
A wonderful book, *Nudge* displays how incentives, especially from government, can encourage better decisions.

Video
Rosling, Hans (2010) *The Magic Washing Machine*: TED Talk: https://www.youtube.com/ watch?v=BZoKfap4g4w
When Rosling describes the magic of a washing machine through its impact on a woman's life, he is telling the bigger story of technology and development.

Rosling, Hans (2007) *The Best Stats You've Ever Seen*: TED Talk: https://www.ted.com/talks/ hans_rosling_the_best_stats_ you_ve_ever_seen?langua ge=en
Taking us through millennia, Rosling tells a long development story very briefly and memorably.

Chapter 12
Economic Growth and Externalities

Books
Banerjee Abhijit and Duflo, Esther (2019) *Good Economics For Hard Times*: Hachette Book Group.
From their global perspective, for topics that range from climate change to connectivity and free trade, Banerjee and Duflo informally share their very readable experiences, opinions, and the facts.

Bremmer, Ian (2022) *The Power of Crisis How Three Threats—And Our Response—Will Change the World*: Simon & Schuster.
A narrative that takes us to the big ideas we can contemplate as we ponder the future.

Deaton, Angus (2013) *The Great Escape: Health, Wealth, and the Origins of Inequality*: Princeton University Press.
Somewhat dated, still, any book or article from Angus Deaton is worth reading because his facts and ideas always remain relevant.

Podcasts
A *Planet Money* talk with Elinor Ostrom: https://www. podcasts.com/npr_planet_ money_podcast/episode/108_ planet_money_elinor_ostrom_ checks_in
Through this podcast we get to know Elinor Ostrom. Just before receiving her Nobel Memorial Economics Prize, she answered questions from her home about her ideas.

The Climate Question BBC podcasts: https://www.bbc. co.uk/programmes/w13xtvb6
A weekly podcast series that focuses on understanding and dealing with climate change through stories from around the world.

INDEX

PICTURE CREDITS